KING JAMES'S SCHOOL, KNARESBOROUGH:

1616 - 2003

Arnold Kellett

Published by
King James's School
Knaresborough

ISBN No 0-9545195-0-7

Designed and printed by
Maxiprint
York, England
www.maxiprint.co.uk

*Dedicated to the memory of Richard F Watts,
Head of History from 1958 to 1984, co-author
of the first history of King James's Grammar
School in 1966.*

King James the First, shown in regal splendour, holding orb and sceptre. Painting by Paul van Somer.

(The Royal Collection © 2003, Her Majesty the Queen)

Contents

Author's Preface and Acknowledgements

Published in the year of the 400th anniversary of King James's accession to the throne of England (1603), this is an account of a school that is proud to bear his name. The project was initiated some time ago by the Headmaster, Dr Hudson, and at last it has materialised, to appear in a year of historical significance.

Anyone who writes the history of a long-established institution like this, inevitably benefits from the labours of others. In this respect I am indebted, first of all, to my former teaching colleagues, Richard Watts and Margaret Hunt, for their *King James's Grammar School* (1966). Richard, a former distinguished Head of History, who died in September 2002, had been invited by the Headmaster, Mr Brewin, to write an account of the school to celebrate its 350th anniversary. He was always rightly proud of what he and Margaret produced, 'sweating blood', he once told me, as they did the hard spade-work of digging out the history of the school from the obscurity of incomplete records and scanty sources.

As they wrote about the Grammar School from its foundation to modern times, it might be argued that I should not cover this period myself, but start where they left off in 1966. Well, quite apart from the fact that it is standard practice in historical writing to go over old ground, perhaps taking a different approach (otherwise there would only ever be one book on any particular topic) my brief has been to give an account of the whole evolution of King James's, and show the contemporary school in the context of its long tradition. I shall therefore start at the beginning, in 1616, but touch more on additional, local aspects of the period covered by that first history, which readers are warmly recommended to read for themselves for further detail.

Secondly, there is another precursor in F R Treadgold's *Challoner's* (1624-1974), which contains interesting material about our founder and our fellow school at Amersham in Buckinghamshire. Both schools have preserved the founder's name – in our case as the title of the school magazine, which incidentally, in more recent issues, uses the original family spelling (with one 'l') *The Chaloner.* I have also been in touch with Judith Curthoys, archivist of Chaloner's old college of Christ Church, Oxford, who has kindly let me see the entry she has written on our founder for the forthcoming *Oxford Dictionary of National Biography.* I have even been in correspondence with a relation of the parson who became Headmaster in 1800 and later absconded with the school papers – an unlikely skeleton in this lady's family cupboard.

I fortunately have a complete set of the *Challoner/Chaloner* school magazines, and as these have chronicled school life (with two longish breaks) from 1932 until the present, they have been a valuable source of information. Then there have been details which have turned up in various documents and publications from the seventeenth century onwards, and I am glad to acknowledge the helpfulness, once again, of the solicitors, Powell, Eddison, Freeman and Wilks, guardians of the 1616 Charter, school rules and other early material. The school rules, incidentally, were usefully transcribed by Mr Watts and members of his LVI history set in 1972.

Over the years, I have taken and collected a number of photographs. Others have been provided by Peter Finan, Head of History, in charge of the school archives, assistance in the use of which has been helpfully given by Lyn Constantine. Other pictures and items have been provided by Messrs O Blakeborough, M Boothroyd, P E Kearney, F Newbould, M Padget, A Prest, J Roper, J Varley, D Watkins, Staunch Design, the *Knaresborough Post* and the *Yorkshire Post.* I might add that the three-reel history I made of the school in old 8mm colour film in the 1970s, as well as Mr Brackenbury's black-and-white film of the school in the late

1950s and early videos, have also been grist to the mill. Atmosphere has even been provided by artefacts of about a century ago which I once rescued when they were being thrown out during a clearance – a push-button desk bell, for example, which must have called many an assembly to attention, and a sturdy teacher's chair, a low-back Windsor (there used to be one in every classroom), in which I sit as I write.

Above all, there has been the evidence provided by eye-witnesses – many former members of staff (including three Headmasters – Mr Lancefield, Mr Moreton and Mr Forster) and countless numbers of old pupils. I am especially grateful to all these witnesses – too numerous to list – who have been willing to share with me memories of their old school, and who have clarified, verified and filled in awkward gaps in my research. Of those who have kindly read through the text, I would just like to mention a fellow-teacher, Alan Hemsworth, and two of my former pupils who later became teaching-colleagues – Mrs Janice Chatten and Linda Baxter. Linda is now the School Administrator, and with characteristic efficiency has helped to steer the book through its final stages, including proof-reading.

There has not, of course, been space to include everything I have been told (and some items, indeed, are best left to unrecorded oral tradition, especially choice morsels of staff-room humour!). But so much of what appears in these pages has the sound basis of joint testimony. The most pleasurable source is when old pupils gather at reunions, which can be said to keep the bygone school alive. For example, one of our daughters, Rachel, who left in 1976, meets with seven school friends several times a year, when they often exchange reminiscences about King James's. Incidentally, to give an account of the alumni, recording all the interesting careers and lives of former pupils, though in a sense part of the history, is a mammoth task, and best left to recording and continual updating by computer. Another aspect of the school is tragic loss through early death. Though such pupils, including some who had recently left, are mostly not recorded here, they are a part of our history, and are remembered with affection by their contemporaries.

I have naturally drawn on my own memories of the school – confirmed by a complete set of mark-books, time-tables, copies of reports, notices, programmes, notebooks, letters, and even the comic verse I used to write for staff leaving-parties. My involvement as a teacher was, in fact, from January 1956 until July 1983. Our three daughters and son all attended King James's, and, partly through them, I have kept in touch with many others who are thankful for their education here. It has been a challenging business putting this all together – like doing a gigantic jigsaw puzzle, with pieces missing or faded and ill-fitting. But out of all the complexity of discontinuous records and imperfect memories, a picture has finally emerged – and though it may well have its deficiencies I can only say that I have done my best.

On the principle that people are far more interesting than things, I have referred to as many individuals as possible. Inevitably these tend to be headmasters and prominent, long-serving teachers. Yet, all the time I have been writing, I have been conscious of the fact that the very backbone of the school has been that valiant body of unnamed teachers who, over the years, have toiled away at the chalk face, as we used to call it, with few free periods, long and exhausting hours of class-contact, and a motivation that has nothing to do with career prospects, but everything to do with a love of learning and a love of children.

I have also been aware that this, like all schools, is a microcosm, a little world within itself. It cannot, of course, escape being influenced by changes in society, especially those in recent decades, when children have experienced the greater freedom, affluence and expectations that would have astonished the lads of 1616. But the influence is reciprocal. And because attitudes and standards are often superior in schools to those of surrounding society, the story of King James's can be seen as one long campaign for the best that can be achieved in intellectual and cultural development, and in recreation and relationships. It may not always have succeeded, but this is the lead the school has always tried to give, a golden strand running through all the ups and downs of its long life. And how satisfying it is to have a single secondary school for the whole town, adding to Knaresborough's sense of identity. The historical significance will, of course, be best appreciated by those who read these chapters through, as a continuous narrative, rather than dip into them.

Finally, this could be regarded as just another of my investigations into local history, once again patiently word-processed by Pat, my wife and indispensable team-mate. But this is obviously far more personal than anything I have written on Knaresborough before, and I have tried to discipline and restrain myself in order to produce an account which I hope will be seen as reasonably objective. To produce this book has been a rare privilege. Here is a school which has added a distinctive facet to the diamond of historic Knaresborough, and will surely continue to do so through this millennium and beyond.

Arnold Kellett,
Knaresborough, 2003.

1. Knaresborough in 1616

What a contrast between the Knaresborough we know today and the town at the time of the school's foundation! The difference is not simply a matter of noting the absence in the early seventeenth century of everyday facilities we take for granted – clean water at the turn of a tap, gas and electricity, varied and abundant food, effective medical treatment, rapid transport, radio, television and all the rest. . . It is that the scale and atmosphere of Knaresborough would have surprised us, and in many ways appealed to us.

The most striking difference is that it was then so much smaller, a compact market town, extending roughly from Gracious Street (a name derived from Anglo-Saxon *gracht hus*, referring to houses on the edge of the town's open sewer) and Briggate, then down High Street to Bond End (the boundary of the 'free borough' in Knaresborough's Charter of 1310) and along the bank of the River Nidd.

The population was correspondingly small. The whole of England around 1600 numbered little more than 4 million. Knaresborough would have had around a thousand inhabitants, but it was certainly growing during this period, as is indicated by the fact that between 1601 and 1620 the parish register shows 252 more baptisms than burials.

The three main focal points of the town were the Parish Church of St John the Baptist, the Market Place and the Castle. The Church was built on ground consecrated in pre-Norman times, as we can conclude from the Viking street-name of Kirkgate ('the way to the church') and the existence of the Anglo-Viking Knaresborough Cross, a section of which can be seen in St Peter's Church at East Marton. The present building includes Norman features in the tower and east end. By 1616, when the first King James's School was taking shape in a house on the eastern fringe of the churchyard, the Church would look rather different from what we see today. The tower would be the same, its attractive little candle-snuffer spire having been added in about 1520. But it would have looked much taller, because the roof of the nave was then lower, and was not raised to its original thirteenth-century height until the Victorian restoration.

Another difference in the setting of the school in 1616 was that the churchyard below it was already filling up with graves, the green space provided by clearance and landscaping only dating from 1973. To the left there would be a view of the thatched cottages on the other side of Kirkgate, especially those on the steep cobbled hill of Waterbag Bank, so called because much of the town's water-supply was brought up here from the river – in leather waterbags strung across the backs of horses and donkeys, or in pails carried by women at a half-penny a time. These water-suppliers, constantly toiling up and down the hill, must have been a familiar sight to the boys of the school – until about 1764, when an Act of Parliament made provision for water to be pumped up to the town from the weir.

At the top of Kirkgate you entered the cobbled Market Place, busy with traders and shoppers and folk gathering round the market cross to exchange news and gossip. There would still be the bull-ring here in 1616, a reminder of the days of rough sports such as bull-baiting and cockfighting, and even rougher justice, with lawbreakers displayed for public ridicule and abuse in the town stocks and pillory.

Townsfolk and people from the surrounding villages would crowd here during Knaresborough's four annual fairs, as well as every Wednesday for market day, which had first been mentioned in 1206, in the reign of King John. When Knaresborough was visited around 1538 by John Leland, Henry VIII's antiquary, he described the market as 'quick' (lively). It was certainly of commercial importance. By 1616 the sale of locally-grown liquorice was being replaced by that of another Knaresborough speciality, cherries, and later, according to Hargrove, this became the biggest corn market in the whole of Yorkshire. Also traded in the market – though direct sales were going on all the time – would be linen, already being produced in great quantities in Knaresborough's expanding cottage industry. The demand for cloth at this time was considerable, not only to supply Knaresborough's own increasing population, but to contribute to export, of which fabric formed by far the biggest proportion in Stuart England. So the economy of the town could be said to be based principally on farming and textiles, the latter including various related trades such as flax-dressing and dyeing – and also on supplying fresh food and other items to the garrison in the very heart of the town.

In 1616 Knaresborough Castle was still to be seen in its original splendour – a mighty fortified residence, on one side with its panoramic view of the Nidd gorge, some 120 feet below, and on the other the barbican gate, whose towers with portcullis grooves remain, and which are pictured in the town's seal used in the school's own coat-of-arms. John Leland had been most impressed by the dozen towers and great keep, noting: 'The Castel standeth magnificently and strongly on a Rok, and hath a very depe diche, hewn out of the Rok, where it is not defendid with the ryver of Nidde'. This ditch, or dry moat, had, in fact, been dug out for King John, who developed and strengthened the Castle between 1204 and 1212, turning it into a munitions centre producing many thousands of quarrels (crossbow bolts), using it as a base for hunting in the Forest of Knaresborough, and presenting the first known Royal Maundy here to thirteen Knaresborough paupers in 1210.

In 1616, with no sign of the upheaval of the Civil War, which would within thirty years lead to the systematic demolition of the Castle, its imposing and impregnable structure must have dominated and reassured the town. Its royal associations would have been remembered with a sense of pride – the granting of a Charter by Edward II in 1310, the complete rebuilding of John's castle for the King's favourite, Piers Gaveston, in 1312, the residence of Edward III and Queen Philippa, and the granting of the Castle and Honour of Knaresborough to their son, John of Gaunt, Duke of Lancaster, in 1372, since which time it has been part of the Duchy of Lancaster.

This historic occasion would certainly have been recalled in 1616, because it was in this year that James I not only granted Knaresborough a school in his name but also granted to his son the lordship of Knaresborough, nine years before he came to the throne as Charles I.

Particularly loyal to the Stuarts were members of the Slingsby family of Scriven, one of whom, Sir Henry Slingsby, was Knaresborough's Member of Parliament at this time. It was, in fact, a member of the same family, William Slingsby, who in about 1571 had discovered the Tewit Well on Harrogate's Stray and had encouraged visitors to come and 'take the waters'. As a result, a small but increasing part of Knaresborough's economy was the spa trade. Each summer its inns were providing accommodation for health-seekers who used the town as a base for visiting the mineral wells around which was later developed the town of Harrogate.

In the first book to be written on this area, *Spadacrene Anglica* (1626), Dr Edmund Deane of York devotes his first chapter to an account of Knaresborough as an excellent place for spa visitors to stay. Indeed, throughout the seventeenth century the town was known as 'Knaresborough Spaw'. Deane's description is worth quoting, as it gives us an idea of the image Knaresborough presented in the early years of King James's School:

> A very ancient Market towne. . . fenced on the South and West parts with the River Nid, which is beautiful here, with two fair bridges of stone. About the towne are divers fruitful valleyes, well replenished with grasse, corne and wood. The waters there are wholesome and cleare, the ayre dry and pure. In brief, there is nothing wanting that may fitly serve for a good and commodious habitation, and the content and entertainment of strangers.

Deane certainly did a good job as an early spin-doctor, but such publicity concealed the fact that Knaresborough was no paradise. Like other market towns, it would have been noisy and smelly, with rat-infested open sewers, and the menace of epidemics of plague and smallpox never far away. And what of education in those days? Can it be assumed that the founding of a school in Knaresborough was like planting a missionary outpost in a wilderness of ignorance and illiteracy?

There is no reason to suppose that Knaresborough was any different from the rest of the country, where it has been estimated (by counting signatures, as distinct from crosses) that around 1600 only about a third of the male population – and far fewer women – could read and write. Literate people, some actually owning books, were mostly the landed gentry, merchants, shopkeepers, clergymen and professional men, such as physicians, apothecaries and teachers. However, this does not mean that the majority – Knaresborough's farm workers, hecklers, spinners and weavers of flax, manual labourers, tradesmen and craftsmen – necessarily experienced any sense of social or cultural deprivation. Their everyday tasks, as well as much of their entertainment, bypassed any need for literacy. They would, for example, enjoy the musicians, strolling players, jugglers, puppeteers, quacks, street vendors and gypsies at the markets and fairs, or they would take part in local customs. These ranged from sword dancing in January, through Hoketide on Easter Sunday (when men stole women's shoes, followed by the women taking their hats), to St Crispin's on the 25th October, the feast day observed by Knaresborough's remarkable number of cordwainers or shoemakers.

It would be a mistake to imagine that our forebears in the early seventeenth century led a dull and deprived life. There must have been, in spite of hardships and premature death, lots of fun – or the Puritans would have had nothing to protest against. And, in addition to a lively communal life there was at least the possibility of cultural refinement. The many Knaresborians who attended the Parish Church would be regularly exposed to the majestic prose of Cranmer in the Book of Common Prayer, and to the unsurpassed English of the new translation of the Bible authorised by King James. It was, in fact, an emphasis on the importance of reading and understanding the Scriptures that gave an impetus to the provision of basic education. Many a child learnt to read and write thanks to tuition from rectors, vicars and curates. Much of this Anglican teaching was done in the church itself, commonly in the church porch. Some clergymen with both enterprise and financial resources went further, and like our Dr Chaloner, founded actual schools.

Teaching, though closely linked with the Church, was not confined to the clergy, and Knaresborough, like other substantial market towns, would have had one or two 'petty schools', or 'dame schools', conducted by lay people teaching small groups of young children in a private house. Here, for a fee, children could receive elementary tuition in reading and writing, perhaps with sufficient arithmetic to enable them to keep accounts.

A minority of wealthy people, of course, ensured that their children, sons especially, were educated by private tutors, and then sent abroad to broaden their outlook. Typical of these, was Sir William Slingsby of Scriven Hall, who in 1610 told his son on leaving home for the grand tour that would strengthen his education, to be careful of the company he kept, 'for the frenche are of an ill conversacon and full of many loathsome deseases'.

For the general population there would certainly have been, long before 1616, several men licensed to teach in Knaresborough, but they were often unreliable and ill qualified, and teaching was so poorly paid that it was typical for only about a fifth of schoolmasters to be doing the work full-time. This no doubt explains why a Knaresborough schoolmaster named John Steward, at the age of 48, started dabbling in the occult in an attempt to find buried treasure, and in 1510 was charged with witchcraft at an ecclesiastical court in York. In evidence against him it was stated that he had kept three bumble-bees under a stone, had called them forth one by one and fed each of them 'with a drope of blode of his fyngor'. To this early example of vampirism, construed as feeding witches' familiars, was added the damning evidence that Steward had used holy water to baptise a cockerel, cat and other creatures. He presumably stole his holy water from the font of Knaresborough Parish Church. If you think this sounds far-fetched, look at the ponderous font-cover, a later replacement of one locked into position to prevent similar acts of sacrilegious theft.

Steward was found guilty, but managed to escape being hanged as a witch or burnt as a heretic – the punishment with which Mother Shipton, living in York, was threatened by Cardinal Wolsey in 1530. Steward's punishment was excommunication, followed by his having to walk round the market places of Knaresborough and other towns carrying a banner displaying a confession of his blasphemies.

Of all the teachers that Knaresborough has known in its long history (and there have been some odd characters amongst us!) I would say that John Steward deserves recognition for colourful originality. And his case at least serves to show the need for a stable and well-conducted school in Knaresborough where, as we shall see, particular emphasis was placed on appointing a master who was no blasphemous heretic, but an upright member of the Church of England.

Blasphemy and heresy were major preoccupations as the Elizabethan period merged into that of the Stuarts. The smooth course of sound Christian doctrine, between what was seen as the extreme of witchcraft on the one hand, and the extreme of Catholicism on the other, was a special concern of the new monarch, King James, and it is characteristic of the atmosphere in which the school which bears his name was founded.

2. King James the First

Whether we speak of 'King James School', or, more correctly, using the possessive, 'King James's School' (because it was his in the sense that it was his foundation) the name of this king is on everybody's lips. And yet we scarcely give a thought to James himself. What do we know about this man who bequeathed his name to the school and is the ground of its very existence?

First, he was a Scot, and because James is a common name in Scotland, it is not surprising that when he became a monarch he was James the Sixth in Scotland before becoming James the First in England. By general consent he adapted well to his new country, surely the first eminent Scot to illustrate Dr Johnson's later dictum that the 'noblest prospect a Scotsman ever sees is the high road that leads him to England'!

During the Royal Progress from Edinburgh the new king was given popular acclaim and even rapturous welcome. He reached York on the 16 April 1603. As he had stayed for a while at Ripley Castle he almost certainly came to York by travelling through Knaresborough, whose Charter, incidentally, he confirmed the following year. I imagine him riding with his escort past Bond End, and up High Street – passing quite close to both sites of the school. In York he was met at Skip Bridge by the sheriffs, a hundred citizens and sixty gentlemen on horseback. They escorted him to Micklegate Bar, where he was welcomed by the Lord Mayor and twelve aldermen in scarlet robes. The Mayor presented to James the keys of the city, led him under a canopy held by six lords to a special service in the Minster, then gave him lavish hospitality at the King's Manor.

Yet, as a contemporary observed, in spite of all this adulation King James remained 'an honest plain Scotsman'. He was, in fact, of the old Stewart dynasty, the name, through the influence of French, which has no 'w', commonly being spelt Stuart.

The second most important thing we should remember about him is that he lived in an age of violent religious controversy. He was born in Edinburgh Castle on 19 June 1566, to Mary Stuart, better known as Mary Queen of Scots, a devout Catholic, whose claim to the English throne was vehemently opposed by the Protestant Elizabeth I. As a result, Mary spent much of her later life imprisoned in various castles (though not Knaresborough Castle) and was convicted of treason and beheaded in 1587, when James was twenty. Following the intrigue surrounding the murder of her husband, Lord Darnley, in 1567, Mary had been forced to abdicate in favour of her infant son, who was crowned James VI of Scotland in a Protestant service at Stirling Castle – when he was thirteen months old. This explains his nickname, 'the Cradle King'.

James was given a thorough classical education supervised by the brilliant scholar George Buchanan, whose curriculum of Latin, Greek and biblical studies, was not unlike the one later to be followed by the first pupils of King James's Grammar School in Knaresborough. The young king proved to be an excellent pupil himself, showing considerable ability as a linguist. By the age of eight he could apparently translate at sight a chapter from the Latin Bible into French, and then into English. He had a particular interest in religion and became something of a theologian. His general grasp of academic matters, together with an active mind and a ready wit, led to the comment by the French King Henri IV that he was 'the wisest fool in Christendom'. In other words, in spite of his impressive wit and general intelligence he showed little common sense when it came to matters of statesmanship. An outstanding example of this was his failure in 1618, two years after the foundation of the school, to prevent the unjust and long-delayed execution of Sir Walter Raleigh.

It is true that various weaknesses and peculiarities were noted in James. Even at the age of eighteen it had been observed that he was ill at ease when not out hunting. Whereas he could

Portrait of King James at the head of his Charter (1616) founding the school.

sit in the saddle for as long as six hours at a time, he could hardly sit still in company. Though he was capable of intelligent conversation, penetrating questions and vigorous debate, he had rough manners, especially in the presence of women, and took no pleasure in either music or dancing. He showed no interest in courtly refinement, especially in matters of dress, and (contemporary King James's ambassadors, please note) he particularly detested earrings in men!

Though he seems to have had few of the social graces associated with royalty, he could be a good host, with jovial conversation, provided it was with a small number. Large crowds, especially when people were queuing up to flatter him, made him lose patience. On one occasion, when he was told his loyal subjects only wanted to see his face, the King is said to have cried out: 'God's Wounds! I will pull down my breeches, and they shall also see my arse!'

The most unflattering description of King James comes from the spiteful pen of Sir Anthony Weldon, who had a pathological hatred of the Scots, on whom he wrote a bitter satire which cost him his job as Clerk of the Green Court. Weldon not only gave a caricature of James, but depicted him during the declining years of old age, when he is known to have suffered from gout, arthritis and kidney disease. (It has been suggested that he suffered from the same hereditary disease, porphyria, that later afflicted his descendant, George III). The King, said Weldon, had a tongue too big for his mouth, which 'made him drink very uncomely, as if eating his drink', with the result that he dribbled. His awkward gait was naturally seized upon, with the additional information that he was for ever fiddling with his codpiece.

Weldon confirmed what others had noticed in telling us that James had favourites (notably the handsome young Earl of Buckingham) whom he could change at a whim. On the positive side he conceded that he was a good deadpan wit and that apart from occasional binges, which he always regretted, he was moderate in diet and drink. His skin, he said, was as soft as silk . . . But this, he mischievously added, was because King James never washed his hands, but 'only rubbed his finger ends slightly with the wet end of a napkin!'

Biographers of James generally placed little value on Weldon's account, though its influence can be seen in the pop-history view neatly satirised in *1066 And All That* . . . 'King James slobbered at the mouth and had favourites. He was thus, a Bad King'.

A strongly prejudiced attitude to James can be seen in some of the Catholics associated with the Gunpowder Plot. One, for example, writing from exile in Spain, refers to him as this 'miserable Scot' and 'this stinking King of ours'. Yet, in surprising contradiction to the charge of being unwashed and smelly, James was passionately opposed to a filthy practice the Plotters were known to indulge in – the new craze of tobacco-smoking. He even wrote a little book about it called *A Counter-Blaste to Tobacco* (1604), in which he attacked smoking as a pernicious habit, dangerous to health, anticipating in a remarkable way modern anti-smoking propaganda. It was, he wrote, 'a custom loathsome to the eye, hateful to the nose, harmful to the brain' – and most perceptive and prophetic of all – 'dangerous to the lungs'.

Much of what King James wrote in an attempt to dissuade his subjects from smoking could be applied to modern society. For example, his observation that we take up smoking and persist with it, mainly because we are influenced by our peers, is one that modern young smokers (yes, even at King James's School!) might well take to heart:

> We cannot be content unless we imitate everything that our fellows do, and so prove ourselves capable of everything that they are capable, like Apes, counterfeiting the manners of others to our destruction.

Another of the practical measures he took to attempt to influence life in England was his encouragement of the silk industry. As the silk worm depends on mulberry trees he arranged for a number of these to be introduced and planted in various parts of the country. A reputation for rather eccentric interests such as this made it easy to accept the story that King James was once so pleased with a joint of roast beef that he took out his sword and knighted it, dubbing it 'Sir Loyne' – though the same anecdote has also been told of Henry VIII and Charles II (and the word 'sirloin' did not originate in this way, but is simply the French *sur longe*).

On a more serious level, it is worth noting that King James made an important contribution to scholarship and literature. In addition to his patronage of writers like Ben Jonson, Shakespeare and John Donne, he initiated and carried through a new translation of the Bible, the masterly Authorised Version. Expressly written in the plain English of the day, it was produced by a team of more than fifty scholars at Oxford, Cambridge and Westminster, 'newly translated out of the Original tongues, and with the Translations diligently compared and revised by his Majesties special Commandment'. It is worth remembering that this, the greatest Christian classic in English, was published in 1611, just five years before the foundation of the school.

This was not the first publication through which King James had sought to promote sound Christian doctrine. He had already written a tract attacking the fashionable practice of witchcraft. In his *Daemonologie* (1597) he outlined and condemned the various devices of the Devil, basing much of it on his personal interviewing of the hostile witches of North Berwick, who in 1590 had met to raise a storm in the North Sea. This was an attempt to wreck his ship as he sailed back to Scotland with his bride, Princess Anne, teenage daughter of the King of Denmark, with whom James, in fact, experienced romantic love and a fruitful marriage, in spite of estrangement in later life.

The most relevant thing about James as far as the school is concerned is that his death was later plotted, not by witches, but by rebellious Catholics, infuriated by the King's failure to implement the tolerance he had promised. Indeed, it could be argued that if there had not been a Gunpowder Plot, there might not have been a King James's School – and yet if the Plot had succeeded, of course, there would have been no King James to found the school. Because the leader of the conspirators, Robert Catesby, was from Warwickshire, it is not always appreciated how much Yorkshire contributed to the Plot, especially this part of Lower Nidderdale, where six out of seven of the principal plotters had once lived or had relatives. Guy Fawkes himself, though born in York in 1570 and brought up a Protestant, had moved to Scotton, just outside Knaresborough, following his father's death and his mother's second marriage, this time to Dennis Bainbridge, a devout Catholic.

Guy settled in Scotton at the homes of his step-father (Percy House and Scotton Old Hall) with his mother and two sisters, when he was seventeen or eighteen, later signing himself in legal documents 'Guy Fawkes of Scotton. . . gentilman'. He must have known Knaresborough well, and through the influence of Catholic relations in the town and surrounding district he became a convert – and like many a convert, a zealot, leaving England at the age of 23 to join the Spanish army then fighting the Protestant armies in the Netherlands. After distinguished service he had by 1603 been promoted Captain Guido Fawkes, and was soon recruited by the Plotters because of his expertise in the use of gunpowder. Under the alias of Johnson, servant of Thomas Percy, he smuggled 36 barrels of gunpowder into a cellar under the House of Lords, but was arrested – just before midnight – on the eve of the famous Fifth of November 1605, when King James was to have opened Parliament.

Guy Fawkes, sketched by Peter Kearney. Was Guy the catalyst who speeded up the school's foundation?

When James heard that the terrorist had been caught red-handed, with lantern, watch, tinder-box and slow fuses, 'booted and spurred', ready to make his get-away, he ordered Fawkes to be brought to his bed-chamber. Here, at 4 o'clock in the morning King James interviewed him, just as he had interviewed the murderous witches of North Berwick. When he asked him, almost in disbelief, how he could have contemplated 'so hideous a treason', which would have caused not only the death of the King, but that of the royal children, Fawkes made his famous reply that 'dangerous diseases require desperate remedies'. James had a particular horror of death by gunpowder, his own father having been strangled just before his home was blown up. So he naturally took a keen personal interest in Guy Fawkes, but treated him with reasonable fairness, ordering that in the Tower of London they should first use the 'gentler tortures' on him (the tightening of manacles) before they had recourse to the rack.

Guy Fawkes courageously held out under torture for four days before finally revealing the names of his fellow-conspirators, most of whom had by that time been rounded up or killed. He not only suffered the traitor's death of being hanged, drawn and quartered, but also the annual disgrace of being burnt in effigy every Bonfire Night (or 'Plot', as it is called in parts of Yorkshire) except at St Peter's School, York, and in Scotton. (Rather odd, incidentally, that there has apparently never been a school bonfire with the ceremonial burning of Guy, celebrating his failure to destroy our royal founder). The sense of outrage was deeply felt by the whole nation, who now said a special prayer of thanksgiving for the King's deliverance every Sunday. James himself issued an official account of the Gunpowder Plot and its providential discovery, and must still have been sensitive about Guy Fawkes even eleven years later when he was approached by one of his Canons of Windsor, the Reverend Dr Robert Chaloner, requesting that he might found a school in the King's name in Knaresborough.

Permission was granted in record time – in just under three weeks. It is not too fanciful to suggest that the reason permission was so readily granted was that it occurred to James that here was an opportunity to found a school in the very area where Guy Fawkes had once lived. James had, after all, stayed with the Catholic Ingilby family at Ripley and must have passed close to Scotton, as well as through Knaresborough. From what we know of him there would have been a certain appeal in having his name perpetuated in a place suspected of Catholic sympathies.

The least we can say is that his giving of his name to the school in 1616 would be no empty formality. King James took a pride in the attachment of his name to an institution – as is indicated by the fact that the following year, in 1617, he insisted that the University of Edinburgh, whose Charter he had granted in 1582, should be known as 'King James's College'. Other northern schools to whom he granted a Charter were at Bishop Auckland (1604) and Almondbury (1608), the only other King James's School in Yorkshire. We should note, however, that he had also founded a school in Otley in 1607, Prince Henry's Grammar School, in the name of his eldest son.

Once our own Charter was granted it is not known whether King James took any further interest in the school. Not that the school ever seems to have taken much interest in him – not until 1966, that is, when a school coat-of-arms was designed and registered, which incorporated heraldic references to him. Then, from September 1971, the new school uniform started to display the Stuart tartan throughout the district – a nice ironical touch. It is as though we now have a perpetual reminder of the failure of a local lad to destroy the Scottish King.

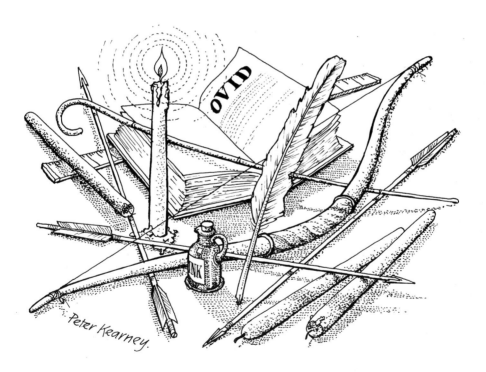

Typical items in use at the first King James's School.

3. The Seventeenth Century: Chaloner's Free Grammar School

The founder of King James's School impressed his stamp on it so unmistakably that it could easily have been called 'Dr Chaloner's School', the official name of the other grammar school founded in the name of the Reverend Doctor Robert Chaloner in Amersham in 1624. As we have seen, there was good reason for King James to have his own name firmly planted in Knaresborough. The full title of the school here was:

Libera Schola Grammaticalis Regis Jacobi in Knaresborough ex fundatione Roberti Chaloner, Sacrae Theologiae Doctoris

The Free Grammar School of King James, of the Foundation of Robert Chaloner, Doctor of Divinity.

The royal link with the school is plainly declared in all the early documents and endorsed by the miniature portrait of King James which heads the Charter, but there is no doubt that Chaloner was the principal figure. He was not simply the man who thought it would be a good idea to give Knaresborough its own grammar school, but one who seems to have taken a personal interest in its establishment and development, down to every detail of its organisation and curriculum.

Something of Chaloner's motivation for founding a school can be gleaned from the Letters Patent (written up as the Charter) granted by King James, in which it is stated that 'Doctor Robert Chaloner, a native of Gouldesborough'

of his own pious desire and good disposition for the education, teaching and instruction of Boys and Youth of the Parishes of Knaresborough and Gouldesborough aforesaid and of others whomsoever, as well poor as rich, intends to found and establish a Free Grammar School in the Town of Knaresborough. . .

Goldsborough was more important in those days, with Goldsborough Hall the seat of Sir Richard Hutton, but was nothing like the size of Knaresborough, and it seems odd that it should have been designated as one of the two catchment areas. The explanation is that this is where Chaloner was born in 1547, though he was, in fact, the second son of Robert and Ann Chaloner of 'Llanfellin' (probably modern Llanfyllin, Powys) and his association with that part of Wales explains why he later received a studentship at Christ Church College, Oxford, which held land there.

Chaloner's intention was to provide education for boys in the Yorkshire district he knew well, and especially for those from families who would not be able to afford private education. The 'free' in the school's title meant what it said, because no fees were to be paid by parishioners of Knaresborough and Goldsborough. Pupils from outside these parishes, however, were apparently regarded as potential fee-payers, and from them the Master was permitted to 'take such stipend as with reason he can get (except they be of kindred of the Founder)'. This last statement confirms that Chaloner, though he had settled in Buckinghamshire from about 1566, still had strong family connections with Yorkshire.

The Chaloners have a distinguished record of service to the nation. Sir Thomas Chaloner (1521-1565), soldier, diplomat and scholar, was knighted on the battlefield of Musselburgh (1547) and in 1557 was elected Member of Parliament for Knaresborough. A link with Buckinghamshire was established when he was granted the manor of Steeple Claydon. His son, Sir Thomas Chaloner the younger (1561-1615), was a pioneer of chemistry and industrial development, opening the first alum mines in England on the family estate at Guisborough. For this he was excommunicated, having angered the Pope by imitating what he had seen on a visit to the alum works at the Vatican. He also experimented with saltpetre, and in 1607 put on a spectacular Twelfth Night firework display for the Court of King James.

It is Sir Thomas Chaloner the younger's friendship with James I which has a special relevance, helping to explain the readiness with which the King granted this distant relation, Robert Chaloner, his request to found a school. Sir Thomas had, in 1603, accompanied James on his Royal Progress from Scotland to his coronation in London. The same year he was appointed as tutor to the King's eldest son, Prince Henry, and accompanied him to Oxford before the boy's tragic death from typhoid in 1612. A further example of his interest in education was his benefaction to St Bee's School in Cumbria.

Our own Robert Chaloner was apparently descended from the same great-great grandfather as Sir Thomas the younger. Though details of his early life remain obscure we can be sure from the university records that in 1564 he went to Christ Church, Oxford, gaining his BA degree in 1566, his MA in 1569, his BD in 1576 and his DD in 1584.

His progress in the Church of England was no less impressive than his academic achievements. In 1566, he was appointed Rector of Fleet Marston in Buckinghamshire. Then in 1576 he was appointed Rector of Amersham, the presentation being made by the Duke of Bedford. The same year he married Christina Garbrand, probably the daughter of an Oxford bookseller friend of Chaloner's, who was also Rector of North Crawley.

In 1584, the year he became a Doctor of Divinity, Robert Chaloner was appointed a Canon of Windsor. In this position he enjoyed considerable status, with access to the Court and no doubt to King James himself. Continuing to reside at Amersham, which is only about fifteen miles to the north of Windsor, he lived in style at the rectory. This was a fine two-storey building of sixteen bays set in sixty acres. Here he and Christina entertained high society, including his patron, the Duke of Bedford. They had no children, but many friends, and seem to have led an active social life, no doubt tempered by the Chaloner family motto:

Frugality is the left hand of Fortune, and Diligence the right.

No portrait of Dr Chaloner appears to have survived. Exhaustive enquiries at Oxford, Windsor and Amersham have unfortunately been in vain.

The Canon was a charitable man, taking a special interest in the Poor Knights of Windsor, making bequests to them, as well as choristers and vergers of Windsor, and 'the godly poor' in his will. As we have seen, the Letters Patent granting official permission for the foundation of the Free Grammar School of King James in Knaresborough were issued remarkably promptly, on the 26th October 1616. As soon as confirmation was made by the Master of Requests on the 14th July 1617, a document was drawn up assigning an annual rent of £20 received from Chaloner's land at Wavendon, Buckinghamshire to the Knaresborough school and its sixteen trustees.

The surprisingly small amount of £20, also specified in Canon Chaloner's will, was for the annual stipend of the schoolmaster – a typical figure for the early seventeenth century. It was, in fact, the same as the stipend provided in the same will for the schoolmaster of the grammar school which was to be established in Amersham in 1624, three years after Chaloner's death, and which was named in his honour 'The Free School of Robert Challoner, Doctor of Divinity', later known as 'Dr Challoner's'. The will also makes provision for a lectureship in divinity at Christ Church or, alternatively, for the maintenance at the college of 'three poor scholars' from Amersham, Goldsborough or Knaresborough.

In its early stages the Amersham school must have been similar to the one at Knaresborough, overcoming its difficulties in the spirit indicated by the motto on its later coat-

Knaresborough Parish Church (St John's) with which the school was closely associated in the early years.

of-arms: *Ad astra per aspera,* which could be freely translated 'Through toil and tribulation to the stars'. The modern Challoner's school is still a grammar school for boys only, with about 1,200 pupils.

Dr Chaloner died in May 1621, and was buried in his church of St. Mary's at Amersham. Although he never lived to see the establishment of the school he planned for Amersham, he was able to take a close interest in what was happening in Knaresborough, perhaps even returning to Yorkshire to see it for himself. Progress was immediately made, thanks to a local benefactor, who is easily overlooked. He was Peter Benson, who generously provided as the new school a house with a garden adjoining the churchyard – the site King James's was to occupy until its move to the present site in 1901.

Peter Benson is mentioned in the Charter as one of the school governors, along with other important local men, such as Sir Henry Slingsby of Scriven, Sir Richard Hutton of Goldsborough, Francis Trappes Birnand, the Rev Henry Darniton (Rector of Goldsborough), Thomas Pickering, Thomas Coghill, William Batty, Peter Slingsby, William Flesher, William Roundell, Francis Barroby, William Darniton, Richard Palliser, William Hill and John Busby. Peter Benson is of interest because he was the Borough Bailiff, imposing law and order on the town, especially by sessions of the Borough Court, held in the Tollboth (on the site of Castle Courtyard) with two prison cells beneath. Peter Benson was a man of property and influence, who, by 1611, had acquired at least sixteen burgage houses, important for the voting rights that went with them. One of these was a house in High Street, which is now an inn, whose name and sign appropriately commemorate 'The Borough Bailiff'.

Though the foundation of the school can confidently be given as 1616, it is not clear when it was first in operation in the house provided by Peter Benson. By 1618 we have reference to the first known Master, Thomas Crosbie, whose brief was plainly set out in the 'Ordinances and Lawes'. This is a remarkable document, a well-preserved and easily legible parchment scroll around six feet in total length, dated 6th November 1616. Few schools can have their

King James's Grammar School on its original site overlooking the Parish Church.

original rules and time-table surviving from such an early date, and one of my happiest memories is of being able to show this parchment to Harry Secombe and millions of viewers in a *Highway* programme in 1991.

Dr Chaloner first stated his requirement that the key figure in the school – 'the Schoole-Maister' (ie the Headmaster, later supported by assistant teachers or 'ushers') should be 'a godly, learned, discreet, sober man, and a diligent teacher and observer of these ordinances'. If not, Chaloner added, 'he shall be removed, and a better sought for and placed'. Any such replacement was to be made by the governors and the founder after a six months trial period. It was also decreed that the Master should not be absent for more than two days unless a 'sufficient deputie' took his place – and leave of absence must be approved by at least six of the governors. Because a minority of fee-paying pupils might come from wealthy families it was stressed that the Master should 'take paines with all indifferently, as well poore as rich' – the latter phrase already used in the Letters Patent.

The school day was exacting. The founder decreed that it should start at six o'clock in the morning in summer, seven in winter – though allowance was made for late arrival because of long distances or severe weather. A minority were boarders. Morning school ended at eleven, then was resumed from one until six. The boys assembled for prayers at the beginning and ending of the school day, using a form of service set down by the founder. Everything was to be said 'distinctly and devoutly', the pupils responding to words said by the Master. Sometimes they sang a Psalm, such as the Sixth. This may have been one of the founder's favourites, but it could hardly have given those lads a cheerful start to the day, with its opening lines from a man evidently mortally wounded, in great pain. . . 'O Lord, rebuke me not in Thine anger, neither chasten me in Thy hot displeasure. . . Heal me, for my bones are vexed. . . I am weary with my groaning. . .' A more encouraging start might have been expected from the scripture that Dr Chaloner specified to be read aloud by the boys, Psalm 119. This, celebrating those who worship God and keep all his commandments, is more uplifting. But it consists of 176 verses, constituting by far the longest chapter in the whole of the Bible!

A high moral tone, as well as good order and discipline, including a smart appearance, was to be an essential feature of education at King James's:

> The Maister shall have diligent regard to the manners of his scholars, and see that they come not uncombed, unwashed, ragged or slovenly, but, before all things, he shall severely punish swearing, lying, picking [i.e. of pockets], stealing, fighting and quarrelling, wanton speeche and uncleane behaviour and such like.

Experienced teachers will take this as evidence of how little things have changed over the centuries. Boys will be boys. Disciplining them, however, is nowadays very different from the 1616 instruction to the Master to 'severely punish'. This, of course, implied corporal punishment in the days when a familiar biblical tenet was that to spare the rod was to spoil the child. Dr Chaloner, however, was careful to guard against the abuse of physical punishment, the rod (either a cane, pliant birch-twig, or a bundle of these) being applied to the posterior only for the more serious misdemeanours:

> The Maister shall use no kinde of correction, save with a rod, moderately; except with a thin ferula [a long, flat wooden ruler] upon the hand for a light fault. If he correct without reason and discretion he shall be . . . displaced after admonition.

In spite of this official limitation of corporal punishment we can imagine that in the early years of the school's history many hands were hit and bottoms beaten. When he died in 1685 a former Master at King James's, Thomas Blanchard, left behind books worth £10 – and 'a whip and a cane, value 4 shillings'.

The early King James's was not called a grammar school for nothing. Typical of all such schools there was a fundamental emphasis on every aspect of grammar, both in English and Latin. At the lowest level were 'the petties', pupils who were only just learning to read and write. Then came the First Form, who were immediately introduced to the principles of Latin grammar, with various texts prescribed by Dr Chaloner, such as selected letters of Cicero. No boy was allowed to proceed to the Second Form unless he could write, an important activity now being the written translation of Latin into English and vice versa, as well as the reading of the fables of Aesop, the dialogues of Erasmus and so forth. In the Third Form they read further prescribed classical texts, including Ovid, and were taught how 'to make an Epistle'. In the Fourth Form, more prescribed texts and the writing of verse. In the Fifth and final year came the more difficult texts such as Virgil, Caesar, Demosthenes, Socrates and Hesiod.

An ambitious curriculum, a legacy of the Renaissance, yet narrow and unrealistic by modern standards. It would, however, even if these weighty classical texts were merely dipped into, have produced a better grasp of English in general, with an improvement in handwriting, spelling and style. The old school slates were not much in evidence here. Every morning, for example, the boys were given 'phrases to be gathered and written in little paper-books for the purpose'. Every afternoon they had to 'learne to write a faire hand after the best copies'. In addition, they had to spend time on grammatical rules, on 'diligent construing and parsing', gaining competence in the handling of Latin verbs in their conjugations and tenses and the cases of Latin nouns in a wide range of vocabulary.

Important though Latin was in the seventeenth-century school, high standards in spoken and written English were also envisaged:

> The Schoole-maister shall carefully teach his schollares to pronounce distinctly and diligently [and] to observe the pointe, comma, colon, semicolon and the period.

There is nothing in Dr Chaloner's curriculum to suggest that any kind of science or maths was studied, though elementary arithmetic and simple calculation would have been learnt by the petties. One subject which received almost equal emphasis with grammar was Christian doctrine, the systematic teaching of which was everywhere being encouraged in the Protestant kingdom of King James, and particularly by clergymen like Chaloner who founded schools. From his 'Ordinances and Lawes' we can take it that Number 11 defines King James's as a Church of England school:

Sir Harry Secombe talking to the author about the school rules of 1616, which were then unrolled and shown to the nation on *Highway* (1991).

> Every schollare shall be taught to say and understand (as their capacity will permit) The Ten Commandments, The Belief [i.e. The Apostles' Creed], The Lord's Prayer, the right use of the Sacrament by some effectuall Catechisme.

The teaching of sound Christian doctrine was to be reinforced by regular attendance at the nearby Parish Church. Here services were regarded as supplementary lessons and the boys required to take notes of what they heard.

What must surely have been for those early King James's lads a dreary round of grammar and religion was at least relieved by a games period, grudgingly permitted:

> The Schoole-maister shall not give often leave to his schollares to play, but upon Thursday afternoone or Saturdayes after evening prayers, and their play [is] to be the tossing of a handball, the [? spinning of a] top, or running or shooting. [i.e. with bows and arrows].

Lest the inmates should get any false notion of liberation during these games periods, they were kept on a tight rein by being compelled to speak to each other (above the First Form) only in Latin – both in the school and when at play. If any boy was caught using English he was to be reported to the Master by two monitors, appointed each week. Even more sinister, 'the Schoole-maister shall privily appoint one other monitor'. It was this monitor's job to spy on the other two, in case they missed a boy, who, for example, had committed the offence of blurting out 'Ey up!' instead of '*Cav-e!*' ('Look out!') as he fired his arrow.

Typical of its time, the Free Grammar School of King James was for boys only. It is unfortunate that girls were then held in such low esteem that Dr Chaloner could mention them merely in passing, in the same paragraph as his note on cleanliness of the building:

> 18. The Schoole-maister shall see the Schoole kept very cleane. He shall not receive any Girls into the Schoole.

The final paragraphs of the Ordinances and Lawes make it clear that it was a privilege to have a place at the school. Boys who were found to be 'unapt to learne' were to be removed by their parents if the Governors were satisfied that there had been 'one yeare's paines taken with them to little profit'. Dr Chaloner was in some ways ahead of his time in his insistence on the involvement and the responsibilities of parents:

1. You shall submit your Childe to the discretion of the Schoole-maister to be ordered in all things.

2. You shall finde your Childe sufficient paper inke and pennes, bookes and candles for winter and all other things at any time requisite for the maintenance of his studies.

3. You shall allow your child alwayes a Bowe and arrowes, bowstringe and bracer to exercise shooting.

4. You shall see diligently from time to time that your childe keepe duly th' ordinary hours in coming to the schoole, and in diligent keeping and duly continuing of his studies and learning.

5. You shall be content to receive your child and put him to some profitable occupation if after one year's experience he shall be found unapt to the learning of Grammar.

6. If your childe shall use often to be absent from the schoole, unlesse it be by reason of sickness, he shall be utterly expelled from the schoole.

The most interesting part of this contract with parents is the requirement that they supply all things needful – paper, books, pens and ink – and 'candles for winter'. This shows Chaloner's determination to make his boys use every hour, almost, that God gave them, going to school in pitch darkness in winter and working from seven o'clock by candlelight. An interesting contrast can be seen in the rules of a school at Witney in Oxfordshire (1660) which allowed no candles on the premises and was in session only in daylight hours.

In the absence of evidence to the contrary we can assume that, guided by the principles laid down by the founder, the school got off to a good start under its first Master, Thomas Crosbie, followed by Robert Hill in 1629. Only a few years later came the upheaval of the Civil War, which affected King James's Grammar School in two ways, one related to the impact of the war on Knaresborough itself, the other related to the way the war affected its financial support from the Chaloner estate in Buckinghamshire.

Although there is no doubt that Knaresborough had many inhabitants who sympathised with Oliver Cromwell and the Parliamentarian cause, the Castle was firmly in Royalist hands, having been secured for King Charles in September 1642 by Sir Henry Slingsby, after his expulsion from the Commons, and then handed over to Sir Richard Hutton of Goldsborough. King James's, true to its name, was also at least nominally royalist. There were even furious protests by Thomas Stockdale, the Parliamentarian MP for Knaresborough, that the Royalists had arranged the appointment of the third schoolmaster, Thomas Bateson, 'contrary to the Charter and Rules of Foundation'. Stockdale maintained that Bateson was not only a Royalist, but anti-Protestant, engaged in the teaching of the children of recusants.

The man responsible for Bateman's appointment was Henry Benson MP, the son of Peter Benson, who had provided the school building and garden. It was largely through Stockdale that Benson, who was accused of corrupt practices, was expelled from the Commons and officially 'rendered incapable ever to sit' (ie in Parliament!).

Stockdale did not manage to remove Bateson, and he remained as Master of King James's until 1652. Royalist elements connected with the school must have been heartened when, at the end of June, 1644, Prince Rupert, grandson of James I, arrived in Knaresborough with a large army, including the best cavalry in England, on his way to relieve the siege of York. By the evening of the 2nd July, however, the Royalists had suffered a disastrous defeat by Cromwell and his Parliamentarians at the Battle of Marston Moor, only about ten miles from

Knaresborough. After various bloody clashes, including the failure of the King's Horse from Knaresborough to raise the siege of Helmsley Castle, the Parliamentarian army finally moved to surround Knaresborough on the 12th November. The siege of the Castle started in earnest at the beginning of December under Colonel John Lilburn, the man later in conflict with Cromwell as the leader of the Levellers.

If the school was still in session, just before the start of the Christmas break, the boys would have had the unique experience of lessons disturbed by the sound of Lilburn's cannon bombarding the Castle.

Boys at the school in 1616. Reconstruction during the Millennium Pageant at Knaresborough Castle. From left Ashley Cavnor, Alasdair White, Jonathan Watts, Paul Morrison.

They would perhaps see the Roundhead soldiers marching and manoeuvering and may well have witnessed their wounded being carried into the nearby Parish Church, where, according to tradition they also stabled their horses. Once the Castle was taken, after various bloody skirmishes, on the 20th December 1644, Knaresborough's royal associations would have seemed at an end, particularly when the Castle was officially and systematically demolished in 1648, and Cromwell himself stayed at a house in High Street.

The Civil War must have had a disturbing effect on the little Grammar School, as well as on the town as a whole. So much had changed, including the Vicar, in those days so closely connected with the school. In June 1645 the incumbent, presumably a Royalist, was replaced, the democratic nature of the decision being stressed in a note in the Parish Register: 'Matthew Booth was admitted to the Vicarage of Knaresborough and elected Minister, by the resignation of Mr Roger Ateye and the free choice of the people.'

Another consequence of the Civil War was that it affected the income from the Chaloner estate in Buckinghamshire on which King James's School depended. Payment of the rent was irregular, and soon in arrears. But the real problems arose when, in 1658, the Wavendon land was bought by a London merchant and speculator, Gifford Bale. He proved to be difficult and devious, the financial awkwardness dragging on until 1676, when he was finally compelled by law to assign the land to the school trustees of Amersham and Knaresborough.

We might conjecture that the Knaresborough school, when passing through this first period of financial insecurity, received support from well-wishers in the town, keen to retain their Grammar School. Although the royal Castle was now dismantled there was, from 1660, the Restoration of the monarchy under Charles II, with the Knaresborough boys no doubt observing Royal Oak Day on the 29th May (the anniversary of the King's triumphant return to London) by wearing a sprig of oak leaf. Some also carried a bunch of nettles with which they hit the bare legs of any who failed to display this symbolic support of the King. Then they would live through the period of a strengthened Catholic cause, with the accession of James II in 1685, then see the pendulum swing back to a stable Protestant monarchy in 1688, dramatically announced in Knaresborough, when Sir Henry Goodricke of Ribston Hall marched into the assembled Borough Court, drew his sword and proclaimed William of Orange as King. Perhaps it would have been pointed out to the boys of the Grammar School that the new King William III was the great-grandson of King James.

4. The Eighteenth Century: Survival and Consolidation

This will be a short chapter, mainly because – for a reason which will be mentioned later – there is a lack of documentary evidence concerning the school during this period. This is also true of Chaloner's School in Amersham, where almost nothing is known of how it fared in the 1700s. In his history F R Treadgold comments: 'This dearth of information is not surprising, for the eighteenth century was an uninspired time as regards secondary education.' He speaks of many masters who simply lived on their endowments and neglected their pupils, the only enterprising work being carried on by charity schools and small private establishments.

This was certainly the case in Knaresborough. An example can be taken from the little autobiography left by the famous Blind Jack of Knaresborough. Born in 1717, John Metcalf was blinded by smallpox at the age of six. But this was after his parents, 'working people' of modest means, had put him to school at the age of four. So at least he started with the advantage, we can assume, of having been taught to write and to 'cypher', a flair for calculation being one of his assets in later life as a road-builder. As Jack was born very close to the Grammar School, in a cottage whose garden adjoined the churchyard, it is conceivable that he was taught there as one of the 'petties'. But, as these were usually no younger than seven or eight it is more likely that he went to one of several dame schools in the town.

Schools for very young children would offer no competition to King James's, but there were others with places for pupils of secondary age. The best-known of these was at the top of High Street in the cobbled enclosure of Park Square. This was a small private school run by the most notorious of all Knaresborough schoolmasters, Eugene Aram. He had been born at Ramsgill in 1704, the son of Peter Aram, a pioneering gardener at Newby Hall and later at Ripley. Encouraged by his father to embark on an ambitious programme of self-education, Eugene became an expert in many subjects, including maths and history, but especially languages. After working as a private tutor, mainly at Gouthwaite Hall, he came to teach in Knaresborough in 1734.

Aram's involvement in crime probably stemmed from the fact that his school was next door to the heckling shop of the flax-dresser Richard Houseman. With Houseman and a young shoemaker called Daniel Clark he set up a fraudulent scheme, which led to the acquisition of a small fortune in goods and jewellery. When Clark disappeared in February 1744 it was assumed that he had absconded with the defrauded valuables. It was not until some fourteen years later, in August 1758, that Houseman confessed he had seen the schoolmaster murder Clark at St Robert's Cave, where the skeleton was found at his direction. Aram, then teaching in King's Lynn, was arrested, tried at York Assizes the following year and condemned to be hanged, then hung in chains on the Knaresborough gibbet.

The relevance of Eugene Aram (and here I have just given the bare bones of the story) is that the school he conducted in Knaresborough for about ten years must have been a rival to the Grammar School. It is significant that although the Vicar, the Rev Thomas Collins, was a governor of King James's School, his own nephew was educated at Aram's school. Evidence that at least some of Aram's pupils were well-educated is contained in the story recorded by a Victorian apologist, Norrison Scatcherd, that after Aram's conviction two of his former pupils came to seek out Houseman, who had turned King's Evidence against their old teacher. Accusing Houseman of being the actual murderer of Clark, they broke his windows and smashed up his furniture. The significant point is that they were now both students with places at Oxford.

It was perhaps the success of private schools like Aram's that persuaded the governors of

The early setting of the Grammar School, situated at the far side of the Parish Church (lower roof before Victorian restoration). To the right is Knaresborough Workhouse (1737).

King James's Grammar School that they would have to do better. The house provided by Peter Benson in 1616 was by this time presumably in need of extensive repair, and too small for the needs of the school. It was therefore decided to rebuild on the same site. Development might have been suggested or encouraged by a substantial new building which had appeared at the other side of the churchyard, the Knaresborough Workhouse, built in 1737 to accommodate 40 paupers, looked after by a Master paid £26.15s. a year. This eventually became a far busier place than the school. 'They come from all parts of the world to Knaresborough', wrote the Master. 'For they know where they get much made on. Pox take 'em all!'

The neat school building we see overlooking the church today (originally with one storey) was opened in 1741, a fact commemorated in a plaque placed by Knaresborough Historical Society in September 1978. No documents concerning this new schoolhouse appear to have survived, but over the door an inscribed stone declared to those who could understand Latin (Eugene Aram would have read it with particular interest!) that the Grammar School had been erected by public subscription:

Hoc Gymnasium Impensis
Collatitiis extructum fuit
Anno Domini MDCCXLI

A few years later the school would be touched by the turbulence which, like the Civil War a hundred years earlier, occurred in mid-century. This was the Jacobite rebellion of 1745. Knaresborough became a recruiting-centre for a kind of mobile Dad's Army, the volunteers raised and trained by Captain William Thornton, who used the charismatic Blind Jack to help recruit the men and then serve as musician, leading the 70 men of 'The Yorkshire Blues' off to

Richardson's Charity School, High Street (1765), later amalgamated with King James's.

Scotland to fight Bonnie Prince Charlie's army. Just as the schoolboys of the previous century had heard of the carnage at Marston Moor in 1644, now their successors heard of the slaughter of the rebels at Culloden in 1746, the victory being celebrated by a special peal of the church bells, deafeningly close to the school.

Though the government was now comparatively stable, in the Age of Reason society was changing rapidly. There was an increased emphasis on the need for education, especially amongst evangelical Christians. There was a move, too, away from the earlier Renaissance preoccupation with Latin and Greek, so that in the school John Wesley founded at Kingswood in 1748, for example, the curriculum included not only the classics and biblical studies but English and French literature, history, maths and 'philosophical experiments' – early science lessons. The influence of Wesley, who preached in Knaresborough several times, and that of the early Methodists, was to be seen in educational work, especially in the following century, with the 'Sabbath and Day School' we shall examine later.

Charitable bequests were being made, such as that of Andrew Holden, who in 1707 left £20 to provide for the poor of Knaresborough and Bond End. But the most important of the charitable donors as far as education is concerned was Thomas Richardson who, in 1765, gave a burgage house and garden at the bottom of High Street, together with £400 in trust, to set up a school. In his will of 1775 he left a further sum of £800, with which the trustees purchased an estate at Follifoot. This yielded a rent of £230 a year which was spent on the master's salary, books, stationery and even the clothing of the school's thirty children, who started at the age of ten. Richardson's Charity School, as it was rightly known, was more forward-looking than the Grammar School in that it took girls as well as boys, and taught them reading, writing and arithmetic, in addition to Christian doctrine. Some of the boys were then started as apprentices.

As the inscription above the door testifies (still clearly legible), other benefactors followed Thomas Richardson, starting with Danson Roundell, who in 1770 gave £42, followed by gifts in the next century that were even more generous. The Master of King James's Grammar School, in spite of his brighter pupils and more academic curriculum, must have looked on enviously at this new school. He was still struggling along on his £20 per annum, while the master at Richardson's had £30, as well as money to spend on teaching materials.

During much of the eighteenth century one of the factors which must have provided a kind of continuity for the school was the exceptionally long incumbency of the Vicar, the Reverend Thomas Collins. He served the parish for 53 years, from 1735 until his death in 1788. During this time he was a school governor and an influential figure in the town, living for the last twenty years of his life in the Collins home of Knaresborough House (from 1952 the home of

Knaresborough Town Council), splendidly situated, with its lawns sweeping down to the Parish Church and the Grammar School. Thomas Collins must have had many happy times, such as his installation of a new peal of eight bells in 1774, followed by the installation of the first known organ in the church. The last four years of his life, however, were clouded by a dispute with the Master of King James's.

This came to light through the research of Richard Watts and Margaret Hunt who relate the sad story of the Rev Anthony Coates, appointed Master in 1770, who was accused by Collins of serious irregularities. This did not apparently happen until 1784, when Coates, having been appointed Rector of Goldsborough, moved to the village, but continued to teach in Knaresborough, walking to the school most days and employing an assistant teacher. A meeting of trustees was called by Collins, at which Coates refused to appear. In his absence he was dismissed from office and his locked chest of school documents ransacked. Coates wrote in protest to the Bishop of Chester: 'I have not had the least altercation with any one single person, except the Rev Mr Collins. . . whose conduct has been so violent as even to take forcible possession of my school and break open the locks therein'. He eventually resigned, around the time that Collins died, aged 84, in August 1788.

At this period the Grammar School would have seemed to the people of Knaresborough a small enclave for a few privileged boys. What about the education of the vast majority of children, including girls? A start had been made at Richardson's Charity School, but an indication of the scale of what remained to be done is given by Hargrove's terse comment:

> Sunday Schools were begun here on the 30th January 1785, when near five hundred children were entered on that truly laudable establishment.

It was the Sunday School movement – started in 1780 by Robert Raikes and a Methodist friend, Sophia Cooke, in Gloucester – that led the way to elementary education for all working-class children, irrespective of ability, and the teaching not only of scriptural knowledge, but reading and writing. Raikes did not launch his important national appeal in John Wesley's *Arminian Magazine* till later in 1785, but already, in the January of that year, almost 500 children in Knaresborough were being taught every Sunday by Anglicans, Methodists and Independents – a number dwarfing the handful of children being taught at King James's, Richardson's and the private schools. This move towards an education for every child, and with a more enlightened curriculum, would be the hallmark of the next century, and speed up the evolution of the Grammar School.

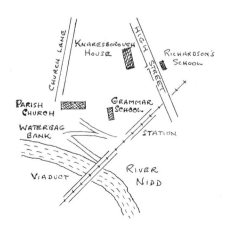

5. The Nineteenth Century: Revival and Reorganisation

The school got off to a bad start in the nineteenth century with the appointment in 1800 of the Rev James Neale as the Master. As Richard Watts and Margaret Hunt have pointed out, the overriding concern of the governors and the Bishop of Chester (in whose diocese Knaresborough was until its transfer to Ripon in 1835) was to ensure that only loyal Anglicans were appointed as heads of the school. They each had to swear the Oath of Supremacy (introduced in 1604) acknowledging the King as Supreme Governor, and accepting the Book of Common Prayer and the liturgy of the Church of England. Academic qualifications and character were apparently given less consideration – though Neale, like his predecessors, had been vouched for by referees.

Whatever his theological soundness, this man – of all the headmasters ever connected with the school – must have infuriated the governors by his neglect and unreliability. A clergyman, originally from Henley, he had a perpetual curacy at Allerton Mauleverer, and was often absent from his teaching duties in Knaresborough – though apparently able to cash in on the Harrogate spa season by teaching children there. In June 1805, after many complaints, he wrote to the secretary of the governors, mentioning the mitigating circumstances, the 'derangement of affairs and illness', which had prevented him from getting to Knaresborough.

The following August he wrote to Robert Stockdale, a trustee and later benefactor of the school: 'I am emboldened to write to you to disperse those foul calumnies with which I have been pursued. On account of my numerous family and small income I have been obliged to contract debts in the neighbourhood on which account I apprehend many reports have been propagated injurious to my character. . .' In his defence Neale added that he had not neglected the school and had even been assisted by two of his sons, both clergymen. One of these sons, the Rev William Neale, later wrote to complain that his father had been unfairly treated by the governors, who had withheld half a year's stipend from him. A nephew of Neale's, William Henry Neale, served as Master of Beverley Grammar School from 1808 to 1815, when he was dismissed by the governors because of the dwindling number of pupils.

In 1809 the Rev James Neale absconded from Knaresborough and moved to Leicestershire, taking all the school papers with him. This was reported by the scandalised churchwardens who said that this had happened after an absence of four months, during which time Neale had made no attempt to provide an usher or any substitute so that 'the teaching of his scholars hath been entirely omitted and the intentions of the Founder frustrated.' Nothing more was discovered concerning the school papers, though Neale wrote to the governors saying he was prepared to swear on oath that he had left them in the school chest. This Master came to an unhappy end, accumulating so many debts in Leicester that he had to flee to London, where he survived on a pittance gained by taking occasional services. Whatever happened to the missing papers, this is the reason for the lamentable lack of information about the school in the eighteenth century and in the early 1800s.

There is no doubt that in the first decades of the nineteenth century the Grammar School was in a precarious state, reduced in 1820, when the Rev William Powell was Master, to only seven fee-paying scholars. Some still had faith in its future, however, including Robert Stockdale, whose legacy of £150 was recorded at a governors' meeting held in 1815, like most such meetings, in the convivial atmosphere of the Crown and Bell, High Street. This legacy later helped to pay for the addition of a second storey to the 1741 building in about 1822. It is interesting to note in these early governors' minutes such additions to their number as

Dr Peter Murray in 1820, the highly-respected founder of Knaresborough's first Free Dispensary of Medicine, originally in Castle Ings. Financial problems were not the only preoccupation of the governors. On the 31st August 1822, for example, they recorded that 'it being found by experience that the Rev Richard Bainbridge, the present Master, is not competent to continue in that office' they were obliged to dismiss him, with the handshake of half a year's salary.

Money was certainly available in the town for educational purposes, but most of it went to children associated with Richardson's School, such as Mrs Alice Shepherd's bequest in 1806 of £3,000 towards 'putting out poor Boys and Girls to useful mechanical Trades', followed by Dr William Craven's addition to this in 1812 of a further £2,000. By 1820 no fewer than 77 Knaresborough children had been apprenticed in this way.

The man who did most to help the less academic children not catered for by the Grammar School was the Vicar who served almost as long as the Rev Thomas Collins. This was the Rev Andrew Cheap, incumbent from 1804 until his death in 1851, during part of which time he served as Chairman of the King James's governors. An outstanding evangelical with a concern to raise standards in the community, he was largely responsible for the building of the first National School in Knaresborough in 1814 on a site close to the Castle, where it can still be seen. Its full title was 'The National School for the Education of the Poor in the Principles of the Established Church'. Like the Grammar School, it was for boys only. Girls were taught in a room adjoining the vicarage until Castle Girls' School was built, opposite the boys' school, in 1837.

An interesting link with those early schools is preserved by a tradition still observed. In 1823 Charles Marshall left £500, the interest from which was to be used to buy clothing for the two boys and two girls who each year were considered 'the best scholars'. I know several old pupils of King James's Grammar School who were the proud recipients of school uniforms (ready for King James's Grammar School) and Stevens Bibles (in memory of Maria Stevens, who died in 1840) when they were at Castle Girls' School in the 1960s. The modern Castle School (Church of England Junior) in Stockwell Road still presents to two boys and two girls an annual cheque as the Marshall Trust Award, and displays the original document describing the bequest.

In 1821 Knaresborough had a population of 5,283, still far greater than that of the infant spa of High Harrogate (1,583) and Low Harrogate (1,010), but these two were rapidly increasing and would eventually coalesce to form a large town. Knaresborough now had a major centre of employment in the old firm of Walton's, who employed at least 200 linen workers. In 1838 Walton's were appointed by Queen Victoria to supply linen to all the royal palaces. In about 1847 they took over the riverside Castle Mill for power spinning and weaving, and in 1851, when they won the Prince Albert Medal at the Great Exhibition, they were employing 272 men, 106 women, 25 boys and 20 girls, the children of their workers being taught at a school in the mill.

From 1823, when an Act of Parliament set up Knaresborough's body of Improvement Commissioners, forerunners of the Urban District Council, there was much tangible evidence of progress – especially the paving, cleansing and lighting of the insanitary streets, the first gaslamps being lit on the 13th September 1824. The addition of another storey to the grammar school was nothing compared with the new buildings going up in the town – the Wesleyan Chapel (1815), the Knaresborough and Claro Savings Bank (1817), St Mary's Catholic Church (1831), the new Court House (1838), Holy Trinity Church (1856), the Town Hall (1862), and the new Congregational Church (1865).

Yet, in spite of increasing Victorian prosperity, King James's Grammar School was only just managing to survive. In 1833, when there was an official Education Enquiry, it could be said to have come at the bottom of the league table. Here is the state of educational play in Knaresborough four years before Victoria came to the throne:

Total number of pupils:

Private Schools	449
National School (Castle Boys)	170
National School (girls)	50
Infants' school	50
Richardson's Charity School	30
King James's Grammar School	24

From this it is clear that there were many small private schools in Knaresborough. Few names have come down to us, but we might mention Thomas Cartwright's school in Gracious Street, where the historian Bishop Stubbs was a pupil, before going to Ripon, and a school where the artist William Powell Frith started at about the age of seven. Later there was the Clarendon House Academy, and the most recent, the Clevedon School, in the Avenue, in the 1940s.

The interesting thing is that the total number of pupils for King James's included four girls – the first time there is a mention of this departure from Dr Chaloner's rule of exclusion. Though the depressing figure of 24 was an increase on the handful recorded a few years earlier, it was short-lived. In 1849 the school, now without a Master, was forced to close down.

It could have been argued that this closure was no great loss to the town, because the movement to educate Knaresborough children in general was gathering momentum. In addition to the more successful schools noted above there was now free basic education provided by the churches, in particular the 100 children being taught by the Catholics and the 170 children (in 1842) being taught in the Sabbath and Day School of the Gracious Street Methodists, whose records note that their pupils were 'mostly children who had no other means of receiving instruction'.

One man, however, felt that something must be done to maintain the teaching of the more academic children, and he came forward, in effect, as the saviour of King James's School. He was Thomas Idell, who had been successfully running a small boarding school in the town. Soon after the closure he readily accepted an invitation by the governors to move his own school into the Grammar School building, with accommodation for his boarders in a house nearby. The governors were so glad to appoint him as the Head Master of the revived grammar school that they were willing to let him run it as a private school, stipulating only that the pupils from Knaresborough and Goldsborough, whom Dr. Chaloner intended to be admitted free, should pay no more than £5 per annum.

This pragmatic solution – less than two years after the closure – led to a happy phase in the history of the school, details of which are given by Richard Watts and Margaret Hunt. They speak of Thomas Idell's efficient administration and his enlightened extension of the curriculum, which now included English, Latin, French, Greek, history, geography, maths, book-keeping, mensuration, physics and natural history. Nevertheless, he remained loyal to the spirit of Dr Chaloner's 'Ordinances and Lawes' by holding morning and evening prayers and using Saturday mornings to teach religious instruction. Soon the school had about 40 pupils, including boarders, and there were assistant and visiting masters. There was, incidentally, little corporal punishment in Idell's school, lines and detention being sufficient to keep the school, according to an official report, 'well-ordered and respected'.

An undated list of school rules from this mid-Victorian period provides an interesting comparison with the first Chaloner rules. For example:

I. The School to be opened every morning at nine o'clock, and the Master, Usher and Scholars to attend until twelve; and again at two o'clock in the afternoon until five.

II. Every Boy is expected to come to School, clean in his person and decent in his apparel, and to be regular and punctual in his attendance.

Any boy absent from prayers was to be given an imposition or corporal punishment, and if absent from school any 'who does not bring a sufficient excuse from his parents in writing is to be treated in every respect as a truant.' Talking in class – the bane of later generations of teachers – was then strictly forbidden once a card had been put up to indicate that study was in progress. The rules, however, concede:

X. That the study card be let down at half-past Ten o' Clock in the Morning; and at half-past Three in the Afternoon, for ten minutes, during which time there shall be a total cessation from work, and any Boy will be allowed to ask his Schoolfellow any necessary question, or go to the door as occasion may require.

XI. In case any Boy wilfully break the two last Rules, by talking, moving from his seat, or not going immediately to work when the study card moves up and the bell rings, for every such offence he shall forfeit one penny.

Thomas Idell was Head Master from 1850 to 1871, his 21 years being only one fewer than the 22 years of Henry Doughty (1653-1675). This long service obviously helped to consolidate the school during the substantial economic changes of the Victorian period. The most noteworthy and symbolic event of the century in Knaresborough was one which might well have literally shaken the school. Around noon on the 11th March 1848 the almost-completed railway viaduct collapsed and fell with a thunderous roar into the river. By the time it was rebuilt, in 1851, the delay in the railway link must have been a factor in Knaresborough not becoming an industrial town, which the success of Walton's linen mill could have led to.

It is worth pausing, in the story of the school, to think about what life must have been like in the Victorian age for the people of Knaresborough. In spite of improvements such as gas lighting, policing, better food supplies and so forth, there was the constant threat of serious disease. The River Nidd was badly polluted. Not only had the lime from the mortar in the collapsed viaduct killed all the fish and flooded Waterside, but by the end of the same year, in October 1848, there was an outbreak of cholera, which eventually led to 38 deaths. This was partly caused by raw sewage still being poured into the river. Even in 1873, when the Improvement Commissioners appointed the town's first medical officer, he immediately drew attention to Knaresborough's dangerous lack of sanitation, with stinking hole-in-the-ground privies close to houses and wells, some of them being used by as many as fifty people.

By this time Knaresborough was being smartened up as far as outward appearance was concerned. In 1872 the Victorian restoration of the Parish Church was completed, with the roof of the nave raised to its original height, crumbling stone replaced, galleries removed and the organ rebuilt. The Church was still very much part of the life of the school which overlooked it, and after Thomas Idell the next two Head Masters were both Anglican parsons, the Rev J G S Nichol and the Rev J N Williams, the latter (1874-78) apparently having introduced as part of the school uniform a kind of square cap – in later years replaced with round caps trimmed with blue and white. Under Williams uniform had to be paid for by parents, who were charged as much as 45 guineas for tuition and boarding fees of the oldest boys (14 to 16 years of age), fees for day-boys being only £1 10 shillings a quarter.

Important developments occurred during the next and quite lengthy headmastership, that of Robert R Harvie (1878-1896), who had taught at the Leeds Mechanics Institute. He had been attracted, along with seven other applicants, by the advert placed in the *Yorkshire Post* and the *School Guardian:*

> Wanted, immediately, MASTER, for the Grammar School at Knaresborough, who is capable of teaching the classics, geography, grammar, writing and arithmetic. The salary is 20 l. per annum, with a commodious school and house capable of accommodating several boarders. A gentleman of experience and ability will find this an eligible situation, the school having been for several years in a flourishing state. . .

Robert Harvie was a good choice. He increased numbers from an average of 40 to 59 day pupils and five boarders, and by 1893 the four girls noted in 1833 had now increased to sixteen. Academic achievement was rewarded at a prizegiving held each December, and we have reports by external examiners from this period showing that standards were high, and improving, one noting that he was pleased to find 'no evidence of Cramming in the School'. The curriculum was now broader, with PT (Physical training) rugby and cricket, Euclid, drawing, even shorthand, alongside the traditional Latin, French, English and maths. There was also some chemistry, as was once appropriately recalled by the venerable pharmacist from the Oldest Chemist's Shop, Mr Edmund Lawrence, who won prizes for chemistry, maths and freehand drawing in 1892. Around the time of his retirement in 1965, when he was in his active nineties, he gave his memories of school to Richard Watts and allowed me to film him showing where he had lined up every day as a pupil to enter the old school building in the days of Mr Harvie. Some indication of the academic success of a school now with an improved scientific curriculum is the fact that three boys at this time went on to study medicine at the Yorkshire College, soon to become the University of Leeds.

The minority of girls in the school, who had been taught separately – the girls upstairs, the boys downstairs – were the forerunners of the truly mixed King James's, which came a step nearer to realisation in 1895. This was the year when a Royal Commission on Secondary Education gave an unfavourable report on the poor state of the old school buildings and the financial struggles of the Head Master. This was followed in October the same year by the decision of the Charity Commission to close down Richardson's Charity School and amalgamate it with King James's Grammar School, which would also absorb the charities of Alice Shepherd and William Craven. In 1867 Richardson's had moved from High Street to a new building opposite the Parish Church (now used as the Parish Hall), mainly through the generosity of a later Rev Thomas Collins (not the Vicar), whose provision of green and yellow uniforms had earned the children of the 'Endowed School' the nickname 'Tommy Collins's canaries' or 'lifeguards'. As Richardson's School had taken both boys and girls from the start, Dr Chaloner's school for boys only was now destined to become a mixed school – though at first there was a separate department for girls.

The Report of the Charity Commission makes interesting reading. For the first time it was declared that no master appointed to the staff needed to be 'in Holy Orders'. The connection with the Church of England, whose doctrines were still to be systematically taught in the school, was further weakened by the provision for pupils to be withdrawn from all such lessons and school prayers at the request of a parent or guardian. In addition to the non-compulsory religious education other subjects were specified. As well as the arts subjects, still including Latin, and maths, there was to be:

> At least one modern Foreign European Language
> Natural Science, with experimental teaching
> Drawing
> Vocal Music
> Drill, or other physical excercises.

The Foundation Governors, a body dating from the Charter of 1616, were to continue, but without any involvement in the running of the school. This was now undertaken by a new Board of fifteen governors, who envisaged that King James's would henceforth provide for a total of a hundred boys, including twenty boarders, with girls in addition. Tuition fees were to be a minimum of £6 a year, paid in advance, but twelve scholarships provided free places, maintaining to some extent Dr Chaloner's intention. The Head Master was required to monitor the intake carefully by interview and an entrance exam. This tested each child in 'reading; writing from dictation; sums in the first four simple rules of Arithmetic, with the Multiplication Table'.

Just before the reorganisation the *Knaresborough Almanack* for 1895 (published the previous November) included the following information:

> Royal Grammar School, Vicarage Lane.
> Head Master, Mr Robert Harvie; Head Mistress, Miss Sherbon.

The official title of the reorganised school was not merely 'royal', but 'King James's Grammar School'. The name was now officially associated with the emblem adapted by the newly-formed Knaresborough Urban District Council from a seventeenth-century seal of the Duchy of Lancaster – the barbican gate of the Castle, surmounted by a hand holding a sprig of oak leaf – incorrectly assumed to be a coat-of-arms. Underneath, the school added its motto, a quotation from Psalm 116 in Latin, taken, not from the Vulgate, but from the Latin prayer books of 1670 and 1865:

> *Quid retribuam Domino pro omnibus quae retribuit mihi?*
> *Calicem salutaris accipiam et nomen Domini invocabo.*

> What shall I render unto the Lord for all His benefits towards me?
> I will take the cup of salvation and call upon the name of the Lord.

(Psalm 116, verses 12, 13)

In spite of long searching I have not been able to find out when this motto, with its translation in the King James Version, was first used. It would be satisfying to think that it went back to Chaloner's days, but Psalm 116 is not one of those he refers to, and the Latin version used is later than his time. The least we can say is that he would surely have approved of it. The notion of showing gratitude for benefits received has meaning and value even in a secular age – though if we read the whole Psalm we shall see that the motto has been taken out of its context and made to seem more general. The psalmist, in fact, is thanking God for deliverance from an illness or wound that has almost killed him: 'The sorrows of death compassed me, and the pains of hell gat hold upon me. . . Thou hast delivered my soul from death, mine eyes from tears, and my feet from falling.'

Robert Harvie continued as Head until May 1896, when he retired with a compensatory sum of £50 – small compared with the £300 that had been given, only the previous year, to the former Head Master of Richardson's, James Birch.

The governors at least offered the new Head the reasonable salary of £100 – though a larger sum would have been the equivalent of Dr Chaloner's original endowment of £20. This time they appointed, in contrast to the succession of clergymen or non-graduates like Robert Harvie, a very well-qualified man with sound teaching experience, one of four applicants interviewed in July, 1896. He was H J Tyack Bake, BA, BSc, late Scholar of Jesus College, Cambridge, who had been in charge of maths and military training at the top boys' Scottish boarding school, Trinity College, Glenalmond, west of Perth. Tyack Bake was the kind of name that Dickens might have invented to fit the severe disciplinarian and fearsome figure that this man proved to be. He is the first of King James's headmasters of whom a photograph seems to have survived. In a typically serious Edwardian group, photographed in front of the Head Master's house (now the Sixth Form Centre), we see Mr H J Tyack Bake, bespectacled and moustached, in a kind of clerical gown, holding his mortar board, grimly seated in the midst of his staff and boys, not one of whom gives the slightest hint of being amused.

The problem with Tyack Bake is that one of his pupils, Geoffrey Dennis, who took a first in history at Oxford and in later life became a successful writer, based his novel, *Bloody Mary's* (1934), on a thinly-disguised King James's Grammar School and its all-powerful head. So the question arises as to how much of the tradition that has come down to us about this Head Master is genuine, and how much is coloured by the invention or exaggeration of the novelist. The Head Master he styles 'Paulus Pengelly, MA, DD, (Oxon)' seems to be only loosely based on what he remembered of Tyack Bake, though others who knew the original have confirmed that certain characteristics are veridical – his violent temper and huge physical frame, for example, especially the mighty arm so perfectly adapted to wielding the cane. Here is a sample of how Geoffrey Dennis conceived him in the novel:

> He was feared. Feared for his commanding personality, his size, his power, against which there was no appeal or hope of appeal. . . his strong right arm. Absolute awe encompassed him. . . We trembled at a look, a tone, a word. . . He flogged. He flogged daily and continually; often with justice, often without mercy; for love of it, on principle, out of habit, by way of exercise, to let off steam, that he might express his abounding personality.

Dennis goes on to describe the Head Master's 'four weapons'. His favourite cane was 'Sunny Jim', 'a lithe little fellow laid across the desk at the start of every lesson,' and used so frequently and vigorously that it was regularly broken and replaced. Next came the stouter cane they called 'Caligula', kept in the Head Master's study, all the more horrible because it sometimes 'had to be *fetched* '. Third was 'Aunt Susan', a knobbly stick used especially for public thrashings, and fourth was 'Black Maria', reserved for the most severe beatings of all, some in the study, some in front of the whole school.

This fiction was not far removed from fact. Oral tradition certainly confirms that Tyack Bake was an enthusiastic exponent of corporal punishment, with his three canes, in ascending order of severity, 'Aunt Jane', 'Aunt Maria' and 'Caligula'. On at least one occasion he thrashed a boy till he bled and had to be taken to the doctor. When the parents complained, the Head offered to pay the doctor's bill. On another occasion he caught a boy trying to get into the school tennis courts (changed by Geoffrey Dennis into a boy wriggling through the hedge into the Head's private garden.) Tyack Bake apparently came along with his cane and thrashed him there and then. Because the boy turned out to be not even a member of the school, the Head had to appear before the local magistrate, who fined him a shilling. Within the school, though, he was, like all headmasters in those days, omnipotent and virtually unaccountable.

On the positive side it must be said that Tyack Bake was an efficient teacher, who did much to raise standards, especially in his own subject of maths. In addition to Latin, the curriculum included English literature, French, history, geography, general science and chemistry, as well as music, art, woodwork and metalwork. The school may have been small, but it had quality. In the KJS archives are handsome leather-bound books from this period – library books such as *Natural Philosophy* (1885) and *The Insect World* (1886), and a lovely copy of *Tom Brown's Schooldays,* with the school motto embossed in gilt on the cover, and, inside, the inscription:

> 1898-1899 Thomas Verity (Form III) Special prize for attendance, being the only scholar with an unbroken record for the year.   H J Tyack Bake, Head Master.

Academic work was balanced by a tough army-style PT under Sergeant Pickering, who gave extra punishment drill to boys kept in detention on the half-days of Wednesdays and Saturdays. There must have been a distinctly military atmosphere in the school at this time. The Head had trained cadets at his previous school, and these were the days, we must remember, when the whole nation was preoccupied with the Boer War (1899-1902). Physical fitness through sport was encouraged, with football, and especially cricket. The Head was a keen cricketer – and apparently kept the grass short by grazing sheep on the school field, using his boys to pick up the sheep droppings before the start of a match.

Tyack Bake's most important contribution was to agitate for a new school building. He had obviously found it entirely unsatisfactory to inherit the split site of the old 1741 school and the Parish Hall building. In September 1896 the recently-formed body of governors decided to build a new school, incorporating a house for the Head Master and his family. The envisaged cost was £8,200, partly provided by the County Council of the West Riding, to which Knaresborough then belonged, in the area with the medieval field-name of Long Flat, the present site off York Road, the land bought from the Slingsbys of Scriven Hall.

Tyack Bake was keen on a move, but convinced that it would be better to seek a site between Knaresborough and Starbeck in order to draw pupils from an area with a larger population, and perhaps thwart a proposal to build a grammar school in Harrogate, in addition to private schools such as Ashville College (founded 1877) and Harrogate Ladies College (founded 1893). This was a view shared by the West Riding authority, but the governors went ahead with their plan to build on the York Road site, even though Tyack Bake refused to attend their meetings in protest.

The preference for a site within Knaresborough itself was understandable. Not only would this be true to Dr Chaloner's original intention, but it would also reinforce the image of Knaresborough as a historic town in its own right, not to be absorbed or marginalised by the mushrooming borough of Harrogate, now nearly six times as big as Knaresborough. It is no coincidence that, just before this decision was made, the Improvement Commissioners had been replaced by the Knaresborough Urban District Council, which had 15 elected members and a body of officers to run the town as an independent authority.

In the long-run the decision to keep the school at the heart of town proved to be the right one, and King James's has continued to add to the distinctive character of Knaresborough. Tyack Bake, however, was absolutely right as far as the near future was concerned. The foundation stone was laid by the Hon H E Butler of Nidd Hall, and building started in the last year of the nineteenth century. But serious financial trouble lay ahead, and within half a dozen years the school would close down for the second time in its history.

6. The Twentieth Century: Removal and Rebirth

With remarkably good timing, the school moved to its new site at the start of a new era. On the 22nd January 1901 Queen Victoria died, and the Edwardian era began. It is interesting to read, in a disintegrating copy of the *Harrogate Herald,* of the Proclamation of Edward VII in Knaresborough Market Place, with all the children of the town assembled in a great circle round the officials and 'the masters of King James's Grammar School in their robes.' After a fanfare by four trumpeters the Proclamation was read by the Under Steward of the Honour of Knaresborough, who later alluded to Knaresborough's Charter, granted by Edward II and confirmed by King James.

On the 5th February 1901, a few days later than advertised, because of the national situation, the Earl of Harewood officially opened King James's Grammar School, newly built on the present site. It was a day for celebration. At 1 pm there was a lunch in Knaresborough Town Hall (in the Market Place) for old pupils and friends of the school, with appropriate speeches by the Earl, the Dean of Ripon, County Alderman A Anderton, Dr Bodington, Principal of the Yorkshire College, and Mr John Lloyd Wharton, MP.

Less inclined to celebrate was Mr Tyack Bake. Disappointed though he must have been about not getting the site he wanted, nearer Harrogate, he nevertheless could contemplate the pleasure of moving into this purpose-built, red-brick school, spacious and modern, when contrasted with the old, dingy buildings by the Parish Church.

Much of that first school building can still be traced, especially if we make use of the surviving architect's blue-print. One block, facing York Road, now the basis of the Sixth Form Centre, consisted of the Head Master's house, assembly hall, classrooms, kitchen and dining rooms, with modern indoor WCs or water closets and a back entrance for the children through the 'cap room' – apparently a reference to the minimal school uniform. On the first floor were bedrooms, dormitories and a 'sick room'. Let into the gable end can still be seen a stone tablet on which the school badge and motto have been sculpted, though the large stone, almost at ground level, presumably laid when the building was founded, has been completely eroded.

A separate science block, including laboratories for physics and chemistry, a lecture room, and rooms for woodwork and metalwork, faced the tree-lined narrow, muddy lane, to be called (from 1933) King James Road. In those days the school had a well-favoured rural setting. Opposite were green fields, beyond which could be seen the eighteenth-century Fish Hall (already being called 'Fysche Hall' because of a bogus old-world spelling). At the other side fields stretched away to the south-east, with scarcely a house in sight. To the left could be seen the sparsely-populated town cemetery, to the right the town football ground and cricket ground. At the other side of the top of Aspin Lane, and also further down, were allotment gardens. In the distance, on a really clear day, you could just make out York Minster.

The buildings must have seemed almost too airy and spacious for the small school that now occupied them. Though girls are occasionally referred to, the photograph taken soon after the move to York Road shows only 36 boys. In addition to the Head we see four masters, three of them wearing gowns and holding mortar

Headmaster's bell, with the commemorative key presented to Lord Harewood when he opened the new buildings in 1901.

Disciplinarian Headmaster Mr Tyack Bake, with staff and pupils of King James's Grammar School, soon after the move to the York Road site in 1901. No hint here of anyone being in the least amused!

boards. It is not known which was which, but staff at the school then included Mr Dean (science), Mr Nuttall (languages and English), Mr Cookson (music and general subjects), Mr Bergan (art, woodwork and metalwork), Mr Bell (music), Mr Dicker (arts subjects) – and Mr Crozier (classics), who according to the Watts-Hunt research, had the distinction of later becoming editor of the *Manchester Guardian*.

The masters were certainly talented and well qualified, and the boys had the advantage of being taught in very small groups. But Tyack Bake's Edwardian school laboured under the disadvantage he had foreseen – insufficient local population to make a fee-paying school viable. Within a few years the new Harrogate Grammar School, officially the Municipal Secondary Day School, which had opened with 44 pupils in 1903 (till 1933 at Haywra Crescent in the town centre), was beginning to offer serious competition.

One of the Harrogate pupils who apparently moved from King James's to this new Grammar School is of special interest. He was Donald Bell VC, killed in action 1916. According to Ackrill's *War Souvenir* and the *Harrogate Herald* he passed his scholarship at St Peter's, Harrogate, then came to Knaresborough Grammar School. The problem is that his name does not appear on our memorial to those killed in the First World War. This is probably explained by the fact that he would come to King James's at the age of eleven in 1901, two years after his older brother, William, who is known to have been a pupil here. He then moved to Harrogate Grammar School, when it opened, conveniently near his home, in 1903. In the short time he was here Donald Bell apparently became a member of the First Eleven cricket team and was an excellent all-round sportsman. Later he became a professional footballer, playing for Newcastle United and Bradford Park Avenue – the only professional footballer to gain a VC, it is said. When he volunteered for the army in 1914 he was a teacher at Starbeck Secondary School.

The hard-working, hard-caning Tyack Bake made one last valiant effort to attract more pupils, putting a photograph of the new school building and a prominent advert in

the *Knaresborough Almanack*. But the governors were already coming to the conclusion that financial losses meant that they had no option but to close down the school. They met under the chairmanship of Major Dent on the 4th July 1905, and reluctantly decided on closure – though formal approval for this was not given until June 1907, when the Board of Education authorised compensation of £200 to be paid to Mr Tyack Bake and the sale of the site and school buildings, if an educational use could not be found.

King James's Grammar School, as advertised in the *Knaresborough Almanack* of 1906, by which time it had been forced to close.

The loss of Knaresborough's Grammar School, so soon after its promising new start on the York Road site, must have been a source of dismay for the whole town. The little-used buildings now stood at the entrance to Knaresborough as a conspicuous and embarrassing red-brick white elephant.

Fortunately the Foundation Governors still existed to keep the soul of Chaloner's school alive, and were looking for some way of adaptation and revival. This, when allied to a ground-swell of feeling in the town and the surrounding villages, resulted in petitions being made to the West Riding Education Committee for the re-opening of the school. The request was not for a traditional grammar school, but rather for one with a bias towards agriculture and a range of practical subjects that would be valued by the farming community. If such a school were provided parents would be found willing and able to pay fees for as many as 140 children, it was claimed.

The result was that the West Riding County Council agreed to set up a special sub-committee who would go ahead to re-open the school on these lines. They appointed a new Head Master, Mr G W Hefford, BSc, previously County Science Master for Staffordshire. He was to be paid a salary of £250 a year, rising in increments of £25 to £300. There were, at first, three other members of staff – Mr T Clark, who had a national diploma in agriculture and dairying (1908-12), Miss W F M Kite, BA, who taught English (1908-17), and Miss E H Collins, who was in charge of domestic subjects (1908-41). Various other, non-permanent, teachers would be appointed for subjects such as woodwork, music, art and PT.

The school re-opened on the 6th October 1908 as the Knaresborough Rural Secondary School. The name fitted it well in its position on the fringe of fertile farmland, with a catchment area reaching as far as Great Ouseburn and, in the other direction, even up to Pateley Bridge and Ripon. Though the curriculum was practical, with a view to raising agricultural standards, there was still a connection with the Grammar School, the governors – who had been replaced by the sub-committee – having ensured that there would be foundation scholarships for the children of Knaresborough and Goldsborough, as envisaged by Dr Chaloner. Normal school fees were a guinea a term, and when the school opened there were about sixty pupils – roughly forty boys and twenty girls. Many would have been about eleven, with the intention of staying at school till they were fifteen.

The committee helped to launch the school by providing additional temporary classrooms, several in a large wooden building with a roof of corrugated iron, attached to the main science

Knaresborough Rural Secondary School in 1908, with Mr G W Hefford as Headmaster. Note the caps and collars of an early school uniform.

block by a covered walkway. The laboratories were refurbished and provision made for the study of biology and botany, which from this time was to have a strong place in the school time-table. It is interesting to see how, in the modern King James's School, this attention to rural education has persisted, notably in the school having its own small farm.

One picture is worth a thousand words. Soon after its establishment a photograph was taken of the assembled staff and pupils of the Knaresborough Rural Secondary School. It compares very favourably with the grim group of Tyack Bake's time. There is the same fashionable, non-smiling, expression on every face. But the general effect is much pleasanter, with the girls in their white dresses and blouses, the boys all smart in new school caps and Eton collars. Apart from one lad in a blazer they are all wearing jackets, one open to reveal a waistcoat, complete with watchchain.

Mr Hefford stayed here only four years, moving on to become a school inspector in 1912. But in this short period he got the school off to a splendid start, doubling the number of pupils to well over a hundred. This increase meant that he could take on additional teachers,including Mr J W Heslop, Mr W H Wilkins, Mr G Winterburn and Miss B Karfoot. Of particular interest are Mr S H Leedale, an old boy of King James's, and Mr A E Wright, who served from 1908 until 1939, thus providing continuity for the revived Grammar School of the future.

In 1912 the new Head Master was Mr C W H Greaves, BSc, who had taught in Pwllheli and lectured in horticulture and agriculture for Shropshire County Council. Ideally qualified to lead such a school, he built on the foundation laid by Mr Hefford, maintaining the emphasis on rural studies, including hands-on activities such as bee-keeping, breeding poultry and working in gardens and greenhouses. Anyone inclined to under-rate the importance of this phase of the school's history, regarding it perhaps as little more than a time for the teaching of apprentice farmers' lads or girls who would enter domestic service, might reflect on the fact that one pupil at the school in this period (leaving in 1924), was James Turner, who became

President of the National Farmers' Union in 1945 (at the age of 37) and was knighted in 1949. I remember Sir James returning to present the prizes and address the school at the Speech Day in 1959. He told amusing tales of his time at a school he was proud of – and no doubt they were listened to with special interest by his first Headmaster, Mr Greaves, who was in the audience.

The formidable task faced by Mr Greaves was that it fell to him to keep the school going through the dark days of the First World War. There were many shortages and uncertainties, in particular staff not being available because of military or other forms of service. Of all the harrowing stories that must have circulated in the school concerning the men in the atrocious killing-fields of 1914-1918, the one that would have meant most would perhaps concern the boy who had been at the school for a while, Donald Bell, previously mentioned. Here is the citation (1916) accompanying the award of the Victoria Cross 'for most conspicuous bravery':

> During an attack (by the Green Howards) a very heavy enfilade fire was opened on the attacking company by a hostile machine gun. Second Lieutenant Bell, immediately, and on his own initiative, crept up a communication trench. . . then rushed across the open under heavy fire and attacked the machine gun, shooting the firer with his revolver and destroying the gun and personnel with (Mills) bombs. This very brave act saved many lives and ensured the success of the attack. Five days later this gallant officer lost his life performing a very similar act of bravery.

The Knaresborough War Memorial, in the appropriately military yet peaceful setting in the Castle Grounds, was later to record the names of 156 Knaresborough men killed in action. Not many of these had been educated at King James's School, which, of course, now served a wide catchment area. Donald Bell VC is commemorated at Harrogate Grammar School, where he completed his education. Nine old boys were recorded on the memorial at King James's as having given their lives for King and country in the Great War:

> W Atkinson, R A Brabiner, W Haley, V H Jewett, E Mawtus, T Moody, C Pool, A H Skirrow, N R Wilson.

In spite of wartime difficulties Mr Greaves was able to maintain and improve standards. He continued to provide boarding facilities – something of special benefit to pupils travelling from distant villages – and to the science-based curriculum he added more arts subjects, including French. The bond with the earlier school was never forgotten, and it is interesting to come across various contemporary references to 'the Grammar School', as the buildings, at least, were still known.

Mr Greaves's most important contribution was his far-sighted appointment of teachers who were to give outstanding service to the school, helping with the transition from rural secondary to grammar school status. These included Mr C B Elmhirst (1911-1931) and Mr Benson Smith (1919-1940), with Miss Collins continuing to teach domestic science, and Mr Wright, woodwork.

Four personalities, in particular, were to give much to the future school. First was Miss Doris M Dews (1919-1953), especially valued for her work with junior children, and for many years captain of the school's company of Girl Guides. She had a reputation for insisting on clear and precise speech, perhaps something not unassociated with her deafness. Then there was Mr Rees Price (1921-1948). Known as 'Taffy', and famed for the excellence of his botanical teaching, driven home by well-aimed hefty clouts, he was later appointed Senior Master. Nancy Shipley, a girl at school in those days (later to return to teach as Mrs Beaumont) recalled many years later, during her long retirement: 'You hardly dare breathe in some of the lessons when I was at school in the 1920s. Taffy Price was particularly fierce – and yet he was a marvellous teacher.'

Mr H W Street (1921-1954) was another long-serving member of the establishment who helped to build up the Grammar School. He had a nickname which testified to the return of Latin to the time-table, for he was habitually referred to as 'Strata Street'. When he retired in 1954 he was celebrated for his great versatility – the teaching of history, maths, Latin and French, his involvement in music, including concert-quality singing at school parties, and his prowess on the games field, where his organisation and inspiration of teams won the admiration of so many boys.

No less versatile was 'Fairy', John Fairclough (1914-1952). I remember him coming back, a few years after his retirement, to help out. He was an unforgettable character – short and stocky, dynamic, voluble, with his Roman nose and prominent, all-seeing eyes, always eager to enlighten and instruct, rapidly firing away in his strong Bolton accent. . . He was so versatile that I was never sure of his official subject. When he retired as Senior Master, it was said that it took several members of staff to replace him! Over 38 years Mr Fairclough taught geography, maths, surveying, natural history, and much more, not to mention his enthusiastic promotion of his spare-time pursuits such as bee-keeping and photography. The bee-keeping presumably inspired his references to the birds and the bees, when he included, I have been told, information about sex in his RE lessons. Mr Fairclough's long service included time at the front in the 1914-18 war, when he was wounded in action, rose to the rank of Captain and had the distinction of being awarded the Military Cross. These adventures, dangers and horrors led him to spice his lessons with another subject – 'How the war was won', providing enjoyable digressions which his classes were always happy to encourage. This became such a familiar feature of school life that the kids immortalised it in a little rhyme:

> The War was won by 'Fairy Feet',
> With a little help from 'Strata Street'.

King James's in July 1925, presided over by the Headmaster, Mr A S Robinson, wearing his mortar board. We see to the left of him Miss A Wood and Mr 'Taffey' Price, to the right Miss C M Andrew and Mr 'Fairy' Fairclough. (Central part of a large panorama).

Sometimes known as 'Captain Fairclough', as well as 'Fairy', his army experience proved useful in his keen leadership of the Scout Troop, including the organisation of school camps.

Carefully-kept records, such as the Register of Admissions, testify to the efficient way Mr Greaves ran the school, which, by 1921, had its first successes in the exams of the Northern Universities Joint Board, forerunners of the School Certificate and GCSE of later years. So it was already much more than an ordinary rural secondary school when a new Head Master took over in 1922. He was Mr Arthur Robinson, popularly known as 'Sam' Robinson. With a first-class degree in chemistry at Manchester, where he was proud of having served as an assistant to the famous Nobel prizewinner, Professor E R Rutherford, and experience as Science Master at Merchant Taylor's School, Crosby, Mr Robinson immediately set about laying the foundation for the superb tradition of chemistry-teaching for which the school became renowned. He also brought to the job of Head Master, not only the efficiency of his predecessors, but a charisma and an unrelenting insistence on the highest standards, which make him – by general consent – the most significant Head in the evolution of the school.

Within four years Sam Robinson had turned King James's back into a Grammar School. Starting with 175 pupils (1923), divided into 8 forms, and a staff of 6 'regular' teachers and 4 'occasional' teachers, he gradually increased the intake and improved exam results. That first academic year he had the satisfaction of seeing twelve pupils gain their School Certificate, six with a distinction in chemistry. A very small number compared with the later successes, but enough to start to build up a five-year exam course leading to two years in the Sixth Form, with a view to taking the Higher School Certificate and applying for university scholarships.

Sam Robinson was by no means the kind of Head Master interested only in achieving impressive exam results. This point was emphasised by Dennis Prest, at school during five of those early years. He told me that, far from being obsessed with exams, as he is often represented, Mr Robinson gave absolutely equal attention to the importance of social development and games, constantly reminding the school to play hard as well as work hard. Dennis recalled, for example, that in about 1926, the Head invited the famous cricketer, Herbert Sutcliffe, to talk to the whole school and demonstrate his use of the bat. In addition to supporting a Debating Society and other groups, Sam Robinson encouraged everybody to take part in some kind of sport, his personal skill being demonstrated particularly in hockey and cricket.

Though he kept firm discipline he was never aloof, but always ready to deal with personal problems, give extra coaching in his own time, and write carefully-worded testimonials for leavers. Respected from the start by both staff and pupils, this was the man who would make the name of King James's Grammar School, Knaresborough, known throughout Yorkshire.

7. King James's Grammar School (1926-1950)

1926 is a key date in the history of the school. This was the year when Mr Robinson, with strong support from the town, achieved his ambition of restoring full grammar school status. Already to some extent under Mr Greaves, and more decisively under Mr Robinson, the school was in nature, if not in name, more than an ordinary secondary school. Now, in the year of the General Strike it was officially re-established as King James's Grammar School, the final approval by the Board of Education being given on the 14th July 1926.

The first *Regulations for the Administration* of the school make interesting reading. A new body of 17 governors was to be set up, elected by the following to serve a maximum of three years:

Knaresborough Urban District Council	4
Knaresborough Rural District Council	2
Great Ouseburn Rural District Council	3
West Riding County Council	3
King James's Foundation Governors	4
The University of Leeds	1

It was also stipulated that this number had to include at least two women governors.

The importance of governors, usually working quietly behind the scenes, should not be overlooked. From 1926 the governing body met at least four times a year, and was to keep in close touch with the Local Education Authority of the West Riding County Council, to whom all financial and other important decisions were to be submitted. With the approval of the Authority the governors were to appoint each 'Head Master' (in those days still usually two separate words) who was to sign a declaration to the effect that, if he should be removed from office by the governors, he would hand over to them 'all the property of the school. . . then in my possession, occupation or control'. It looks as though somebody involved in the drafting of the regulations had remembered the case of the earlier Head who had absconded with all the school documents!

In consultation with the governors the Head was responsible for the curriculum, the number of teachers, the length of the term and holidays, and the general organisation, teaching and discipline. Teachers were to be appointed (or dismissed) by the governors in consultation with the Head, each serving a minimum of a term and a maximum of a year on probation. It was to be a co-educational school for children between the ages of 10 and 18. Parents had to sign an agreement to keep their child at the school until at least the term in which the age of 16 was reached. There was to be an entrance exam and tuition fees of not less than nine guineas a year, which covered 'the use of books and stationery'. These fees could be reduced or waived in certain cases, especially through various scholarships and bursaries.

The new governors seem to have given wholehearted support to Mr Robinson in his ambition to make King James's not simply a top-quality Grammar School but one of the best in Yorkshire. Those who were at school at this time have testified to the good order and studious atmosphere. There would soon be a School Song, specially written and composed by two of the staff, but for the present they continued to sing, at the end of each term, the Harrow School Song, 'Forty Years On'. The teachers all wore academic gowns, and the Head Master and staff even wore their mortar boards, not just on special occasions, but each morning when they appeared on the platform before the assembled school, and the Head solemnly called out the opening Latin question of the school motto. There was a school uniform of maroon cap

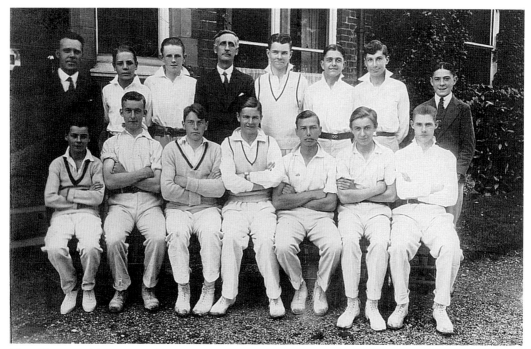

First Eleven Cricket team (1931), taken in front of the house of the Headmaster, who is seen in the centre. To the left is Mr H W Street.

and blazer piped with green, the boys wearing grey trousers and the girls blouses and green skirts. They moved from class to class, not in response to an electric bell, but to the vigorous ringing of a handbell by a prefect walking along the corridors. Persistent or serious offenders had to turn up for a Saturday morning detention, when, in later years, they were required to do menial tasks, such as digging out weeds from the asphalt tennis courts.

Good behaviour and serious study were maintained in spite of the inadequacy of the premises – and an improvement of these was an early priority. Quite apart from the need for more modern facilities, especially for the teaching of science, the sheer increase in numbers meant that a new building was necessary. The 175 pupils of 1923 had now increased to 223 and the school showed every sign of further growth.

While plans were being worked out for new building Mr Robinson could at least deal with the problem of increasing numbers by appointing extra staff. Once again, we see from the length of service how these teachers provided the continuity and stability which has been so noticeable at King James's. Appointments included, for example, Miss Alice Wood, French and Senior Mistress (1923-51), Mr F F Ellis, Head of Maths (1925-46), who in 1929 married a teaching-colleague, Miss E Lancaster, English and French. Another member of staff, Miss C Andrew, Latin (1927-38) also married a fellow member of staff – the Head Master himself, Mr Robinson's first marriage having ended in separation.

Other appointments were Mr S M Barker, science and maths, Miss I G Mailer, English (1925-31), Mr J P Walker, PT (1926-34) and Miss M Craik, French (1929-38). Especially long-serving teachers, familiar institutions to generations of pupils, were Mr Sid Norman, physics (1928-63), nicknamed 'Joe', and Nancy M Shipley, a former pupil, and one of the school's first Oxford graduates, well known as Mrs Nancy Beaumont, a popular teacher of English, returning to teach in 1936 and not retiring until l974. In 1938 Miss Mary M Dixon replaced Miss Craik, teaching French, and also netball and tennis. In later years, as Head of

Modern Languages, she also taught German, marrying in 1960 to become Mrs Wilson. John Metcalfe joined the staff in 1939 as woodwork master, and later qualified to teach RE.

The most remarkable teachers appointed by Sam Robinson were two who eventually were to play a major role in administration, supporting the Head in shaping and leading the school. The first was Miss B M Sawdon, Head of English, better known as 'Molly', appointed in 1935 and retiring at Easter 1973, thus giving the school almost 38 years of dedicated service. Small in physique, mighty in personality, she was a major driving-force in teaching, dramatic production, discipline and the general well-being of the school, especially in her many years as Senior Mistress and Deputy Head. The second was Charles S Walker, who came to teach chemistry in 1939, and who, as a kind of genial parallel to Molly, later became Senior Master, then Deputy Head. 'Whisky' Walker (named after the familiar brand) was young and handsome, and especially popular with the girls. He maintained the high quality of chemistry teaching established here by Sam Robinson and also shared the Head's enthusiasm for cricket. 'Charlie' Walker, like Molly Sawdon, was to play an important part in the re-organisation leading to the Comprehensive School, not retiring until 1975.

In the chronicle of a school it is easy to think only of the various teachers who have formed the core of its existence. Yet we must also pay attention to the non-teaching staff, without whom the school could not have functioned. In these King James's was wonderfully blessed by two distinctive and lovable characters appointed by Sam Robinson – Albert and Maud Scurrah. Maud was originally appointed as housemaid to Mrs Robinson, the Head Master's wife, in 1925. After receiving training from Mrs Robinson, who was apparently an expert in culinary matters, Maud took over as Cook-in-charge, eventually supervising school dinners at King James's for forty years. How clearly we remember her – a white-coated, white-capped, bespectacled figure, short and plump, rapping out orders and occasionally reaching out to clip the ear of any lad misbehaving at table. For many years she presided over the kitchen and dining-room area housed first in the school, then in the successive primitive, functional buildings known as 'the canteen'. For the Sixth Form Christmas party of 1956 I remember composing a rhymed quiz on school characters which included the verse:

> Who is she, who though not very lean,
> Bustles so briskly around the canteen,
> Distributing dishes, delicious but plain,
> And clouting the boys if they dare to complain?
> So let us say grace and give thanks to the Lord
> For the tenpenny banquet provided by Maud!

Two bits of school history are preserved in the last two lines – the fact that school dinners were always preceded by grace, said by a prefect, and the cost of the meals, 10d, equivalent to about 4 pence. When Maud started, she once told me, the dinners cost only half this.

Maud's husband, Albert, was appointed school Caretaker in 1928 – a gruff and formidable Knaresborian who would stand no nonsense from either headmasters, staff or pupils, but with a winning way, a sense of humour – and an expert darts player. Of happy memory, Albert and Maud, with due respect to King James I, were the uncrowned King and Queen of the school.

Unlike Mr Tyack Bake, Mr Robinson seems to have had a good relationship with his governors, and was always grateful for the keen interest shown by the Chairman, Major A E Collins and the Vice Chairman, County Alderman H Eddy, JP. The latter was a successful businessman, with a well-known boot and shoe shop in the market place. His outstanding public service was recognised by the award of an MBE in 1937, and the following year he took over as Chairman of the Governors, having already served as a school governor for 31 years and been partly responsible for the re-opening of the school in 1908. It was said that Councillor Eddy, in order to get things done, had 'made a perfect nuisance of himself' by badgering the authorities. Alderman Eddy's dedication to the school could be said to have been truly cemented when he built his house a matter of yards away at the end of King James Road, calling it 'Eddystone'.

With the support and enthusiasm of governors like Alderman Eddy the much-needed extra building started to materialise. As early as 1928 there had been some rationalisation of the existing space, with accommodation for the boarders, who were now few in number, removed to the Headmaster's house. The real need, of course, was for extensions and new classrooms. The Foundation Governors still had a part to play, and the go-ahead was delayed until the West Riding County Council accepted their offer of rent-free tenancy of the school buildings for the foreseeable future. By the summer of 1933 the extensions were largely completed, and the whole project finished by Easter 1934.

The school now extended handsomely along King James Road, with new laboratories for physics and botany (later the school library), on the ground floor, a domestic science room (later the main entrance), and above these a spacious, well-lit new art-room. There were new classrooms and cloakrooms and, on the ground floor, a large new gymnasium, which also served as a school hall (most of it now forming the school library). The old army hut at the front of the school, divided into three classrooms heated by coke stoves, was removed and converted into sports pavilions. Later there was a hard surface playground at the back of the school, including a tennis court.

The formal opening took place at 3 pm on the 18th September 1933, when Lord Harewood, having been welcomed by a guard of honour of at least fifty Scouts and Guides, was led by Mr Robinson into the new hall/gymnasium, filled to capacity with invited guests, staff and pupils. After a hymn, prayer by the Vicar, Canon H L Ogle, a scriptural reading, and speeches by Major Collins and Lord Harewood, the extensions were formally handed over to the governors on behalf of the County Council, by Sir Percy Jackson. It is not surprising to learn that he thanked the hard-working man who was to become Chairman of the Governors and 'spoke enthusiastically of Mr Eddy's perseverance in the matter, and of his Yorkshire tenacity of purpose'.

Sam Robinson must have been, like his Scouts in their 'Gang Show' song, riding along on the crest of a wave. His glow of pride can still be felt, warming the musty pages of the second issue of the *Challoner,* the school magazine he had started in 1932, which, incidentally, was now describing him in one word as 'Headmaster'. In his School Notes he wrote:

> The school enjoyed a real red letter day on September 18th, when the extensions were opened by Lord Harewood. . . The progress of the school and the excellent work of the pupils during the last ten years were the vital factors in securing the new buildings. Since 1925 we have carried off 21 County Majors, including the top place on more than one occasion and 13 State Scholarships. Record successes were obtained last July in the Higher School Certificate. . . We were the only school under the West Riding Authority to gain ten distinctions. . . The Sixth Form last year was exceptionally brilliant. The pupils worked like Trojans, Romans and Spartans, and our results merely reflect their intrinsic worth.

This reference to three vigorous peoples in ancient history is explained by the fact that Sam Robinson had introduced the house system, dividing the school into Trojans, Spartans and Romans, each new entrant being allocated permanently to a house. Normally the houses – originally separate buildings of a boarding school – competed mainly in sport, but eventually they were expected to vie with each other in academic results.

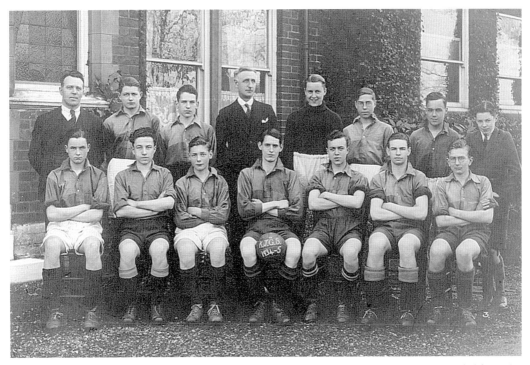

First Eleven Football team (1934-5) with the Headmaster (centre) and Mr 'Strata' Street. Third from the left, next to the Captain, D T Colohan, is the boy later to become the famous wartime pilot, 'Bunny' Clayton.

What is impressive about these exam results – and they were to be maintained and exceeded – was that they came from such a small school, the total number of pupils only having risen, by 1933, to about 320 – though two years later it had increased to a three-form entry.

These early school magazines show that small though the school then was, it had a range of activities which would have done credit to a far larger organisation. Here was no inhuman exam-factory, but a community of young people engaged in healthy pursuits intended to stimulate and develop bodies and souls as well as brains. The three houses competed for a Games Shield as well as a Work Shield, sports results being given prominence in the *Challoner*, with a detailed report of Sports Day, held each July on the 'Top Field'. It is interesting to see that, in addition to events such as the '100 Yards and 220 Yards Scratch' (sprints), 220 and 440 yards handicap, high jump, and long jump, there were girls' skipping, obstacle races, three-legged races, sack races, potato races, chariot races, relay races for boys and girls, tug of war for boys and girls – and, an early indication of what became a special tradition at King James's, so well placed for this sport, the Cross Country. Prizes presented included shields, trophies and, one each for the best boy and girl competitor, the Championship Cup and the Challoner Cup.

As well as athletics the magazine covers the usual games, such as the successes of the First and Second Eleven in football and the girls' hockey team, and not only boys' cricket, with as many as 17 good matches played in the season, but also girls' cricket. This was no gimmick, but taken very seriously by the girls, who provided a detailed report, with batting and bowling averages, just like the boys. A reference, in 1933, to the female cricket team having lost to the Old Girls shows that egalitarian sports were already well-established in the school.

Open-air activities were also a feature of the flourishing company of Guides and troop of Scouts, the former led by Miss Dews, the latter by Messrs Fairclough and Ellis. In 1932 there

'Jolly Hockey-sticks' team of KJGS girls in 1936 in front of the Headmaster's house, Back (from left): P Bosworth, E Gatiss, M Huddleston, M Pickles,W Fryer, Miss M Craik, D Baines; Front: M Cooper, P Thrower, B Clayton, H Moorey, D Kitching.

was a particularly successful Scout camp on the banks of the Derwent near Castle Howard, with patrols taking it in turn to do the cooking, swimming, boating, fishing, shooting, singing songs in the tents and round the camp fire – and listening to the novelty of 'the school wireless'. There was a visitors' day when the Scouts welcomed the Headmaster, parents and friends. Before they struck camp a clock was presented 'as a token of the Scouts' appreciation of the work done by Captain Fairclough'. In subsequent years the annual summer camp was extended to become the School Camp.

Of the indoor 'out of school' activities chronicled in the magazines the two most popular seem to have been the Debating Society and Literary and Dramatic Society, both founded by Mr Ellis as off-shoots of the almost defunct Challoner Society, the first in 1932, the second in 1933. An interesting testimony to the prevalence of encouragement rather than coercion is seen in the very first motion to be debated by a society which was to go on from strength to strength at King James's. Understandably defeated, the motion was: 'That school games should be made compulsory'.

In the early meetings the Dramatic Society simply read plays, but soon these were being performed, at first in school uniform, but eventually in costume, with a minimum of props and scenery, on a stage in the hall/gym at the end nearest the present school entrance. The early reports of the Dramatic Society, incidentally, are signed by Elizabeth Gatiss and M Thwaites, both of whom returned to teach English, the latter well-known as Mrs Maggie Winter.

In addition to insight into work of the teams and societies the school magazines show that life in school was never dull. There are accounts of all kinds of visits, either to the school by a visiting company performing extracts from *Macbeth* or from the school when 'Fairy' took a party to see and sample Rowntrees of York. There is news, too, of old pupils, some only recent leavers, such as the enjoyable account by Nancy Shipley of life at Oxford in the early 1930s. Creative writing also appears at the end of each *Challoner*, some of it soon to be encouraged by Nancy herself. There is verse and prose of a good standard, some of it very original, a few items being entirely in French.

The saddest note in these first journals of King James's is surely the 1938 account of the school's annual visit to the Parish Church for November the Eleventh, Armistice Day. This particular service had been conducted by the Vicar, the Rev Richard A Talbot MC, who had told the children that they were the generation who would be able to reconstruct society, once peace had been truly secured. . . We can imagine how the staff and adults present would feel: the 1914-18 war still so keenly remembered, and now another war with Germany already being contemplated.

As in the First War, the school carried on in spite of all kinds of difficulties. One of these was a shortage of supplies, including paper, so a first casualty was the *Challoner*, which did not reappear again until October 1951. Though we are denied accounts of the war years which would no doubt have enlivened the pages of the school magazine, we can draw on considerable oral history from old pupils. Some remember, for example, the care that had to be taken so as not to waste paper and exercise books, the blacking-out, the criss-crossing of windows with paper tape and other Air Raid Precautions, volunteers from the Sixth Form acting as fire-watchers each night, pupils carrying around gas-masks in those awkward cardboard boxes on string – even the assembling of gas-masks in the gym. In the early months there was considerable moving around to minimise casualties from air raids – the evacuation of Cockburn High School, Leeds, to Knaresborough, which made use of some of the school buildings, and the reception of individual evacuee children, looked after by the Head, Miss Sawdon, Miss Wood and Miss Dixon.

Alma Pratt, as she then was, who was Head Girl shortly after the war, recalls the various ways in which the school made its wartime contribution. In 1942, as part of Warship Week, organised by the National Savings Committee, she had been chosen to represent the Lower School at a competition in Castle Yard with a patriotic speech which won a cup. She remembers how the pupils used to help the war effort by knitting stockings and blankets, removing the carbon rods from used batteries, 'digging for victory' on the school allotments, and going out 'tatie-scratting' on local farms, when the boys were paid ninepence an hour, but the girls only sixpence. More memories of this period were captured in two interesting publications by John Mountain in 1992 and 1994, the latter including a full list of staff and pupils.

Inspired by wartime patriotism, a School Song was introduced in about 1942. The original version of the music was written by Mr Geoffrey Watson, Head of Music (1940-1959). Always known as Professor Watson or 'Prof', he was a charming little gentleman, who in summer could always be seen with a home-grown rose in his button-hole. The words, written by Molly Sawdon, are as follows:

Let us sing in love and duty,
    To our school this song we raise,
Here mid Yorkshire's tranquil beauty,
    Heart and voice we lift in praise.
To each one is freely tendered
    Fellowship and gaiety,
Brighter pathways to the future,
    Vision, opportunity:
    Quid retribuam Domino?

Heir of such a proud tradition,
    Bred in peace and tried in war,
What to help the future total,
    Can I render as my score?
Breadth of mind and, moral courage,
    Humour, kindness, brotherhood
Never-failing zest for service,
    And the pow'r to find life good.
    Haec retribuam Domino

Those who were at school in the post-war years remember singing the School Song at morning assembly – every day!

As a contribution to the war effort certain members of staff left to serve their country, for example, in the Royal Navy (Mr Metcalfe and Mr Whellock) or on secret munitions work with the Ministry of Supply (Mr Walker). On the home front the Home Guard or 'Dad's Army' and the Auxiliary Fire Service made use of the buildings and grounds. In school there was a Girls' Training Company, wearing a uniform of black berets, white blouses and navy-blue skirts. For the boys a branch of the Air Defence Cadets Corps (later the ATC) was also started by Mr Norman, but most prominent of all was the Army Cadet Corps under the command of Captain Fairclough, MC.

Bernard ('Bunny') Clayton DFC, CGM, DSO, famed bomber pilot, educated at King James's Grammar School 1931-38.

'Fairy' was in his element, and pupils have recalled how he was telling his 1914-18 War tales with renewed vigour, and exhibiting artefacts in the little military museum that formed part of his geography room on the bottom corridor. An unusual contribution was made by Mr Kenneth Ford, who taught chemistry here from 1935 to 1939. An influential Quaker pacifist, he joined the Friends Ambulance Unit and was one of the first to enter the Belsen concentration camp.

An important factor in keeping up morale was the quality of school dinners. Sometimes supplementing wartime rations with her own resources Maud always managed to serve up wholesome food, attractive in taste and adequate in quantity. Mouths may still water at the remembrance, for example, of her delicious liver and bacon, followed, say, by her jam roly-poly and custard. Maud's belief that school meals should be pleasurable as well as nourishing was reflected in her saying: 'I know what my bairns like'.

Of the many men educated at the school who served in the armed forces, the best known were two nationally-renowned pilots in the Royal Air Force: 'Bunny' Clayton and 'Ginger' Lacey. Bernard W Clayton, a Boroughbridge lad, was a keen sportsman, an excellent footballer, and when he left in 1938 he won a County Major scholarship, just like his sister did in the same year. As a pilot in the Second World War he proved to be a remarkable all-rounder, serving in Fighter Command, then Bomber Command, soon with the reputation of having flown every kind of aircraft used by the RAF.

Though he did not take part in the famed Dambusters' raid, 'Bunny' joined their 617 Squadron soon afterwards, and his skill and bravery on many dangerous missions led to the award of the Distinguished Service Order, the Distinguished Flying Cross and the Conspicuous Gallantry Medal. He was the only person to be invested by George VI with the DFC and the CGM at the same time and the only RAF man to receive both the the CGM and the DSO. 'Bunny' Clayton was a great hero at school, where many had his autograph, but he was tragically killed not long after the war when he was a passenger in a plane that crashed during a test-flight in 1951.

Even better known was the ace fighter-pilot, 'Ginger' Lacey. He had entered the First Form in 1927, travelling from Wetherby. A fellow-member of his form, the Harrogate architect, the late John Miller, used to tell me how he remembered with affection this lively lad, James Henry Lacey, nicknamed 'Ginger' because of his straggling reddish hair. He apparently had a reputation for pranks and harmless practical jokes – such as when he arranged for an alarm clock, locked in a cupboard, to go off in the middle of an English lesson. Once he put a wasp, which he had first killed, down the blouse of a terrified girl – and was caught in the act by the Senior Mistress, Miss Wood. Lacey should have got good marks in Miss Wood's French lessons, because he copied his homework from one of the top girls – but he always seemed to get lower marks for identical work. More relevant to Lacey's future as a pilot were the subjects he especially enjoyed – chemistry under the Headmaster, physics under Mr Sid Norman, maths under Mr Ferdinand Ellis and geography under Captain Fairclough, of whose Scout troop 'Ginger' was a keen member.

James Harry ('Ginger') Lacey, Battle of Britain ace fighter-pilot, recipient of ten medals, educated at King James's Grammar School 1927-1933.

After a time in the Sixth Form 'Ginger' Lacey worked as a pharmacist in Leeds, then joined the Yorkshire Aeroplane Club at Yeadon and the RAF Volunteer Reserve, where he qualified as a pilot and instructor. During the Second World War he took part in an astonishing total of 87 combats as a fighter pilot. Flying mainly Hurricanes, he had shot down 23 enemy planes by the end of 1940 – more than any other RAF pilot in the Battle of Britain. The planes he destroyed famously included the Heinkel that had bombed Buckingham Palace. Mentioned in dispatches, 'Ginger' was awarded the Croix de Guerre, the Distinguished Flying Medal with Bar, and eight other medals. How wonderful for the school to have produced these real-life heroes, 'Bunny' and 'Ginger', who had helped to save the nation from being invaded by the Nazis!

Whereas 'Ginger' Lacey survived, eventually to enjoy a quiet retirement at Flamborough, of the many King James's old boys who served in the war a remarkable proportion lost their lives. The total number of Knaresborough service personnel killed in the Second World War was 54 , almost a third of the figure for the First War. Yet the number of KJGS old boys killed, 22, was proportionally greater, partly because the school was much bigger. Their names were inscribed on an oak plaque presented by Mr Robinson on his retirement and were later incorporated with the 1914-18 casualties on the plaque presented by Mr Fairclough in 1965. They are:

W H Botterill, R V Cartwright, B C Crossland, R F Fuller, R J Fyfe,
B Hewson, D Holmes, A Houseman, A W Hughes, J J Kirk,
J A Milner, J Mitchell, C L Moore, D Myers, W Panton, D Parker,
K Robinson, C H Smith, J A Taylor, E Wilson, G E Waddington,
V A Wood.

In spite of the euphoria of Victory in Europe Day (8th May 1945) it was a long time before life fully returned to a normality free from rationing and shortages. It was not until 1951 that the publication of the *Challoner* was resumed, the School Notes recording with satisfaction: 'We successfully weathered the war years. . . Academic successes during these [past] twelve years are happily far too many to mention'.

Standards had certainly been kept up in spite of the wartime difficulties. Girls at school in the late 1940s, such as Nancy Buckle, remember the care that was taken to ensure correctness in uniform. Though it was strictly controlled, just a little latitude was allowed. Girls whose families could afford it wore their bottle-green gym-slips with *four* pleats, instead of three, and a velour hat instead of a beret, with a straw boater in summer, both decorated with a green and maroon ribbon.

Maroon was also the colour of the blazers, and the caps worn by the boys. These carried the school badge, also available as a bronze brooch. 'Jock' White (PE and geography), a former Commando, pounced on boys who walked around with hands in pockets, and Miss Wood winkled out any girl brazen enough to have her hair permed.

The biggest post-war changes affecting the school resulted from the 1944 Education Act of R A Butler. From now on there were to be no fee-paying pupils, and no scholarships, though the Foundation Governors could award grants for further studies at college and university. All entrants were to be selected by the 11 plus exam. The Divisional Executive for Education was now set up in Harrogate, far less remote than Wakefield. The governors were reorganised, but fortunately still had as their Chairman Lady Evelyn Collins of Knaresborough House and Kirkman Bank, a cousin of Winston Churchill, who had been awarded an OBE for her hospital work in the First World War. Lady Evelyn took a particular interest in preserving the traditions and reputation of the school.

Another important change decreed by the Ministry of Education was the replacement of the School Certificate and Higher School

Mr A S ('Sam') Robinson, Headmaster of King James's Grammar School from 1922 to 1950.

Certificate with the General Certificate of Education – the GCE at Ordinary Level and Advanced Level. Mr Robinson would easily have coped with this new challenge, but it was now time for him to retire. When this took place in 1950 the first issue of the revived *Challoner* printed a photograph and a tribute which included the comment:

> Retiring headmasters are always said to have been well loved, but 'Sam' *was* loved, and with more reason than many another. The number of old pupils who owe their present position to Mr Robinson must be legion. . . he demanded and gave the best. Shoddy work annoyed and astonished him, because he was incapable of it.

Mr A S Robinson had stamped his personality so firmly on the school that his retirement could be regarded as the end of an era. Yet it was by no means the end of the small Grammar School with a big reputation. It is a tribute to the quality of the foundational Robinson era that King James's would now go on to even greater things.

8. King James's Grammar School (1951-1965)

An obvious cliché to emerge as we relate the story of the school is that Sam Robinson was a hard act to follow. For the autumn term of 1950 the fort was held by Captain Fairclough as acting Headmaster, then Mr Robinson's successor took up his appointment at the beginning of 1951. He was Mr D J Stevens, MA (Cantab), who had taught history at Bedford Modern School. Two other Cambridge men started here in 1952: Richard Beetham, Head of Maths, and Terry Sayles, Head of Geography, both of whom were to give the school long years of service, Mr Sayles later in partnership with the colleague he married, Miss Marjorie Newmarch, who taught English.

Douglas Stevens was Headmaster here for four and a half years, a short period compared with that of his predecessor. This prompted the school magazine later to comment that some of the staff and pupils 'had only just begun to get used to Mr Stevens when they heard he was leaving'. Comparatively short though his stay was, this tall, energetic and cultured Headmaster made his impact.

In addition to maintaining academic standards and aiming at the best results in the new GCE exams, he made a point of developing the social life of the school, in particular starting, in 1952, the Association of Parents and Friends, which eventually led to the PTA or Parents and Teachers Association. This held fund-raising events and a series of talks, one of these being an account of the 'Erratic history of King James's' given by the Headmaster. In this he paid tribute to Mr Robinson who, he said, had re-established the tradition of scholarship and left behind 'a school of great initiative and character'. Mr Stevens, as a historian, valued the school's heritage, including its Latin motto. Pupils in his day remember him in the morning assembly, an imposing figure in his gown, calling out *'Quid retribuam Domino'?* a question in later years to be asked by the Head Boy.

Mr Stevens did much to encourage existing activities, such as games and drama, where the House Drama Competition now alternated with the annual school play. But he was best remembered for his outstanding contribution to music. In this he worked closely with the Head of Music, Geoffrey Watson. A conductor himself, Mr Stevens was keen to start and support a school orchestra. Soon the nucleus of six players had grown to eighteen, and concerts were performed, including contributions by the Senior School Choir, also conducted by the Headmaster, and the Junior Choir, conducted by Mr Watson. As well as a variety of light classics, concerts included choral works such as *Hiawatha's Wedding Feast* by Coleridge Taylor, again conducted by Mr Stevens, and the school took part in the Harrogate Festival. A great boost to the musical prowess of the school came when D P Blakeson became principal trumpet of the National Youth Orchestra and won a scholarship to the Royal College of Music.

Interest in classical music had also been fostered by the Gramophone Society, whose first illustrated talk in 1952 on jazz was given by a pupil, Anthony Burton, in later life a presenter of television documentaries. There was even around this time a popular dance band formed by past and present pupils, and it can be said that the strong musical tradition at King James's, which came to full fruition in the Comprehensive School, has its roots in the stimulus and enterprise of the brief Stevens era.

Another society formed in this period, in September 1951, was the Natural History Society. This had been founded by the Head of Biology, Frank Hodgson, who started here in 1946, moving to become Headmaster of Boroughbridge Secondary Modern School in 1953, when he was replaced by Ian Day. The chairman was Howard Jowsey (appointed in 1949), a man of many talents, who taught arts subjects, mainly English and Latin, yet was an expert botanist, and in later years wrote a book on the flora of the district. The Natural History Society

Mr J D Stevens, Headmaster, conducting the school orchestra in the hall/gym in 1952.

organised regular outings in search of specimens, both close at hand and as far afield as Flamborough and Bempton Cliffs.

School trips abroad, impossible during the war, could now be resumed, and were still something of an adventurous novelty. Miss Dixon, Miss Mackay, and Miss Chew, for example, took school parties to Paris and Haute Savoie in 1952 and 1953, and Miss Dixon and Miss Newmarch took a party to Germany. The first *assistante*, incidentally, appears to have been Monique Besnard in 1953, with a degree from the Sorbonne, beginning the long succession of young ladies (with one or two gentlemen), who have stimulated and guided French conversation.

Interesting news from abroad, as well as from all over the country, came especially from reports of the activities of old pupils published in the *Challoner*. The King James's Grammar School Old Pupils' Association flourished in the early 1950s. In the years 1954-5, for example, when Howard Bell was President and J C A Rathmell the Secretary, there were 400 members receiving circulars of the Association's activities. These included cricket and football matches, various social gatherings and the annual dinner dance at the Cairn Hydro in the December, at which the guest of honour was 'Ginger' Lacey.

Sports Day, 1955, was particularly successful and had the benefit of good weather and a large attendance of parents and friends. The three school houses – Romans (green), Spartans (red) and Trojans (blue) – still competed in a full range of athletic events, now including the mile, javelin and discus, the inter-house relay making an exciting finale. At the close the Chairman of the Governors, Lady Evelyn Collins, presented a dozen cups, shields and awards. The traditional Cross Country had already been held, following a route which ended by going along the river, up the last steps to Crag Lane, then down to the bottom of Aspin Lane and the football field.

Games in general were in a healthy state, with quality matches in cricket, football, hockey, netball, tennis and rounders. Though several members of staff helped to coach, referee and umpire, such as Mr Nudds, Mr Sayles, Mr Lumbers and Miss Newmarch, the overall responsibility belonged to Mr Joe Bertram, appointed to teach boys' PE and games, as well as maths, in 1951, and leaving in 1959, later to become Headmaster of Hunsingore Primary School. Appointed at the same time as Mr Bertram, was the very first full-time mistress to be in charge of girls' PE and games, Miss Chew. When she left in 1955 she was followed for a short while by Miss Yvonne Sewell, an old pupil of the school. Finally, though the Scouts, revived for a while by Messrs Sayles and Nudds, never recovered from the departure of Mr Fairclough, the Guides continued to be active for a further few years, led by Mrs Edna Pinder, formerly Miss Lees, and Miss Jewitt.

All this physical and social activity was balanced by a corresponding excellence on the academic side. The impressive results of the Robinson age were being maintained, as can be judged from external exam results and the number of State Scholarships, County Bursaries and Exhibitions won in the 1950s. (A full list of these, incidentally, can be seen in the appendix of the history by Richard Watts and Margaret Hunt – details all the more valuable in that the school's honours boards, on which they were proudly displayed, were regrettably removed in the late 1970s.)

When Mr Stevens left in 1955, the school was in good fettle – a three-form entry Grammar School, well on the way to a total of nearly 500 pupils, with a Sixth Form of more than 80. The man destined to carry forward this going concern was Mr Frank Brewin, appointed Headmaster from September 1955. He was a well-built, dignified figure, with a physique developed in his student days in tennis, hockey, rowing and cross-country running. He had a domed forehead, horn-rimmed glasses, bristling moustache, and mostly wore the dour and disapproving expression of the classic Headmaster who will stand no nonsense. Throughout his time here he continued to sign his letters in the older two-word style of 'Head Master'.

Born in Derbyshire and educated at Chesterfield Grammar School and Christ's College, Cambridge, he studied maths and physics, to become an MA (Cantab) and BSc (London), followed by teaching experiences at Malton Grammar School and Queen Margaret's, Walsall, becoming Head of Maths at Bedford School in 1943. As members of staff soon realised, Mr Brewin was a keen member of the Church of England, a conservative evangelical, whose ultimate authority in all things was not the government or the West Riding County Council, but the Bible. Not that the new Head could be accused of pushing his religious views down the throats of staff and pupils, but a serious Christian commitment, indeed, a missionary calling to give his whole life to the school, underpinned everything he did. From the start he was a serious and dedicated man, supported in everything by his Scottish wife, Mary, who was always interested and involved, their home being the Headmaster's house in the school itself. Mr Brewin was unswerving and uncompromising in his principles, almost literally using every hour God gave him, in true Chaloner style, for what he saw as the good of the school.

Mr Brewin was, in fact, so different in his approach from previous Headmasters of King James's that a period of adjustment was inevitable. This I experienced at first hand, having joined the staff in January 1956, the start of the new Head's second term – though I had been appointed following an interview by Lady Evelyn Collins and Mr Stevens, the previous summer. As a new boy myself I had, first of all, to make a number of adjustments of my own. I had come here from teaching at Ashville College, Harrogate, a Methodist boys' boarding school. It was a contrast now to teach only day pupils – and to teach girls. What a civilising influence the girls seemed to provide! It took me quite a while, though, to get used to the King James's Grammar School custom of addressing all boys by their surnames, and girls by their Christian names. So it was, for example, Nadine, Gloria, Corinne, Lucille, Myrette. . . but Blakeson, Clough, Triffit, Wiggins, Wox. . . Still, whether boys or girls, I found a more relaxed relationship between staff and pupils, reflected in the fact that whereas at Ashville every master wore a gown, at King James's gowns were now generally no longer worn, except by the Headmaster, who was rarely seen without one. His first office was a very small room at the end of the corridor nearest to his house. Adjoining it was the Secretary's office, occupied by Miss Enid Atkinson, who left in 1957 to become a PE teacher.

As I settled in myself I was very much aware that Mr Brewin was not having an easy ride as he set about imposing his ideas on the highly-qualified and well co-ordinated staff. One of the earliest innovations also involved the way in which people should be addressed. Mr Brewin, understandably following the custom of his previous school, habitually addressed the men teachers by their surnames. So it was 'Sayles', 'Murphy', 'Day', 'Metcalfe', 'Kellett', the courtesy of 'Mr' being systematically denied us, just as the boys were denied their first names. When referred to in writing, especially on the time-table, as was the general custom, we were further reduced to our initials.

The first contentious issue was Mr Brewin's introduction in January 1956 of the School Fund. This received its income mainly by each family with children at school paying in half a crown a term (the equivalent of 12½ pence). The fund was used to provide items over and above the normal provision of the West Riding County Council, such as cups and shields, games teas, the support of school societies and so on. A full balance sheet was regularly published in the *Challoner*. One day after school many of us were in the men's staff-room (then in the middle of the top corridor) vociferously commenting on the first School Fund accounts, which had just appeared on the notice board. In the middle of this the Headmaster entered, sensed the atmosphere, and called out: 'Is Bertram here?' Quick as a flash, Richard Beetham, with mock helpfulness, retorted, 'No, *Bertram's* not here. . . But *Mister* Bertram is!' The Head, taken aback, and perhaps looking for a scapegoat, rounded upon the amiable Raymond Nudds, who happened to be leaning back in his chair with his feet on the table. 'Nudds!', roared Mr Brewin. 'Do you mind?' Mr Nudds calmly replied to the effect that he had not put up his feet especially to insult the Head. . . and somehow an explosive confrontation was defused. . . Adjustments were made – both by the new Head and the staff – and the school moved forward on the next stage of its evolution.

Another thing noticed by the whole school was that morning assembly was now taken very seriously indeed. 'Prayers', as Mr Brewin called this, was a short but formal Christian service in the hall/gymnasium. It was almost always led by the Headmaster himself, in a grey suit and black gown, and he was solemn in tone and manner, with the style of a Puritan. The service included a hymn, prayers and a reading from the Scriptures. (Gideon New Testaments, incidentally, were regularly presented to pupils by Mr Neville Knox, two of whose sons were here.) Mr Brewin, as a good Anglican, also kept up the tradition of having the whole school, every Wednesday morning, declaim the General Thanksgiving from the Book of Common Prayer, a passage every pupil had to learn by heart. It was remarkable to hear nearly 500 children reel off, not only the Lord's Prayer, which in those days every schoolchild knew, but this much longer, more complex passage of seventeenth-century prose. The force and elegance of its style, though, made this something worth learning as a model of good English, irrespective of any religious considerations. Written by a Yorkshireman, Bishop Edward Reynolds (1599-1676), here is the passage learnt, recited – and, in some cases, remembered many years later:

> Almighty God, Father of all mercies, we thine unworthy servants do give thee most humble and hearty thanks for all thy goodness and loving-kindness to us, and to all men. We bless thee for our creation, preservation, and all the blessings of this life; but above all, for thine inestimable love in the redemption of the world by our Lord Jesus Christ; for the means of grace, and for the hope of glory. And, we beseech thee, give us that due sense of all thy mercies, that our hearts may be unfeignedly thankful, and that we show forth thy praise, not only with our lips, but in our lives; by giving up ourselves to thy service, and by walking before thee in holiness and righteousness all our days; through Jesus Christ our Lord, to whom with thee and the Holy Ghost be all honour and glory, world without end. Amen.

In contrast to this was something rather more contemporary in style, read from the front every Friday, the Old Pupils' Prayer. In this we asked a blessing on 'all those who have gone forth from this school to enter upon their several callings in the world. . .' We asked for their protection and guidance, and 'that they may use their talents to the full'. It was a weekly reminder that when they left school they would never entirely sever their connection, and would be prayed for every week during term. In later years Mr Brewin even offered the parents 'NOPED' cards (Nine O'clock Prayer Every Day), inviting them to pray for the school.

Also, in my early years, morning assembly always included a reminder of the School Motto. The Head Boy, usually on Friday, would call out, asking the school what it was going to give back to the Lord for all the blessings he had bestowed:

Quid retribuam Domino, pro omnibus quae retribuit mihi?

To which the whole school replied that it would take the cup of salvation and call on the name of the Lord, bawling out in apparently perfect unison:

Calicem salutaris accipiam, et nomen Domini invocabo!

At least, that's what they were *supposed* to say. From where the staff stood, at the back, it was obvious from the ill-suppressed grins and lack of synchronisation that some of the lads were blithely mouthing their own version. One variant, given to me by Ken Gregson, who had been a pupil in the 1940s, was 'No men domino Greta Garbo!' Informants from the late 1950s confessed that they said, for example, 'No men play dominoes with Sambo!' They had it to a fine art, and their youthful cynicism was all undetected by the Head at the front, who no doubt gained a satisfying impression of promising youthful piety. Some remember how Mr Jowsey, in those days, used his Latin lessons to get them to pronounce the 'v' correctly, as a 'w', so it *should* have sounded 'inwocabo'. Others remember that at one time the Head Boy's reading of the full verse in Latin was followed by an English translation read by the Head Girl.

Like his predecessors, Mr Brewin was determined to promote work and play in equal measure. Evidence for this can be found in his notes of 'Reports to Governors' Meetings' in which he sometimes gives as much space to games results as to exam results. He gave his personal support to games and sport, maintaining the competition between the three school houses. He cannot have been happy, however, with the names of the houses – all referring to the ancient pagans of Rome, Sparta and Troy. Numbers now justified a fourth house, but he decided that an additional name such as 'Chaldeans', 'Babylonians' or 'Phoenicians', would be 'too difficult to shout from the touch line'. So history was made, at the end of the summer term, 1957, when four new school houses replaced the old ones, each name having a local association. They were: Castle, Crag, Forest and Nidd – short and sensible names readily accepted by everybody.

The first sports day in which the new houses competed was in 1958, when Forest won the House Cup, presented by Councillor G A Holch JP, who had become Chairman of Governors in 1956. A great friend of the school, especially during the Brewin years, Albert Holch was also six times Chairman of the Knaresborough Urban District Council, then an Alderman of the Harrogate District, his close association with King James's ending only with his death in 1977.

This 1958 Sports Day was also the first to be held on the 'far field' at the bottom of Aspin Lane, now the ground of Knaresborough Cricket Club. From this time we had the pattern of me being the Sports Day announcer (a job I took over temporarily from Mr Norman – and did for 25 years), white-coated starters with their pistols, especially Mr Watts, Mr Hearld and later Mr Wetherill, and the presentation of trophies, organised by Mr Walker. That July, too, the name 'Swimming Sports' was given to the event held in the Harrogate Swimming Baths, previously known as the 'Swimming Gala'.

The staff of King James's Grammar School, May 1957. Front from left: J Jenkinson, Mrs M Kettlewood, S Norman, Miss B M Sawdon, Mr F Brewin, C S Walker, Miss M Dixon, J Metcalfe, Mrs E Ellis. Middle: Miss Silcox, Mrs N Beaumont, Miss Y Sewell, Mrs M Winter, R Beetham, J Lumbers, H W Jowsey, W P D Murphy, Miss M Newmarch, Mrs E Pinder, Mrs Thrower, Back: G Watson, J Bertram, I Day, T Sayles, A Kellett, P R Nudds. (Everybody is looking at the camera except Mr Sayles. He is looking at Miss Newmarch, whom he was soon to marry).

As he established himself, Mr Brewin made it clear that in addition to aiming for a high standard in work and play, good discipline must be maintained. He was a man of rule and regulation, and eventually issued a Code of Behaviour consisting of fourteen specific rules. These included the usual prohibitions of bad language, bullying, being late, and so forth, but there was a particular emphasis on orderly movement between classrooms, which were never to be entered until the teacher was present. An attempt to control noisy corridor traffic – still one of the great sources of stress in many schools – was made in Rule 3:

> Move along the left-hand side of the corridors, and do not run, shout, whistle or push.

Another indication of how little things have changed was Rule 11:

> Do no drawing, writing or marking on walls, doors, tables or notices.

(One of my all-time favourite graffiti which I saw inscribed in school was '*Hitler lives – and is the Headmaster*'. But I will not disclose under which Headmaster this appeared!)

And the most familiar prohibition of all, Rule 9:

> Do not eat during lesson time. At no time must you have chewing gum or cigarettes in your possession. Chewing gum is forbidden. Do not drop litter.

Not eating in class was one thing, but this rule was extended to 'No eating in the streets'. Many at KJGS during this period will remember that it was regarded as letting the school down if you were caught going around Knaresborough chewing sweets or licking ice-cream – let alone eating fish and chips – horror of horrors! – out of paper, using your fingers! Then, as in later years, there were problems when large numbers of children were released into town during the lunch hour, especially those who were patrons of a popular coffee bar, 'The Grotto', at the corner of Gracious Street and Castlegate, which was a thorn in Mr Brewin's side.

The most cunning device to facilitate eating sweets during lessons was surely the one invented by a lively lad called Russell. I remember suspecting him of eating during one of my French lessons in the third year. When I accused him he automatically opened his mouth wide to prove his innocence and obligingly turned out his pockets. I then noticed a bulky hardback book on his desk and, while the class got on with a written exercise, I casually picked it up and started to turn over the pages. It was *The Young Fur Traders* by R M Ballantyne, innocent enough. After the first few pages I suddenly found I was looking at a quarter of a pound of liquorice allsorts, concealed in the hollowed-out book. Well, I confiscated the vandalised volume and recently showed it to Mr Russell, now a reformed character. He recalled how liquorice allsorts had sustained him in many a lesson and that when he left school Mr Brewin told him he had caned him more than any other single boy – even more than his fellow-villains, Morgan and Gerard.

Mr Brewin, though never in the same league as Mr Tyack Bake, did a lot of caning in his early years at King James's (including the thrashing of a boy who had taken a short cut on a long run – and who later came back as a teacher!). I think most of us on the staff accepted corporal punishment as a final sanction, short of expulsion, to be administered by the Head as a back-up to our own discipline. Mr Brewin, like Miss Sawdon, was a firm disciplinarian himself and would never tolerate talking or silly behaviour. A most effective device of his was to bring the whole assembled school to order by suddenly booming out in a furious voice, 'Stand still!' Nobody ever seemed to be moving at the time, but silence and attention instantly followed – out of sheer astonishment.

Misdemeanours of a less serious nature were dealt with by a small infantry platoon of prefects commanded by a Head Boy and Head Girl. It was a real privilege to be made a prefect, with extra talks and visits known as 'The Prefectorials'. In the 1956 *Challoner* Mr Brewin thanked the prefects and monitors for keeping the school in good order, noting with pleasure that they would be led for a second year by Martin Minogue and Sondra Blackstone as Head Boy and Head Girl. Punishment took the form of either the Prefects' Detention, or the more dreaded staff detention, held on Saturday mornings and after school. In addition, lines or other written impositions were given. Teachers had their individual penalties, and there was also a kind of official school line, which ran as follows, the words having to be written alternately in ink, then pencil – just to add to the torment:

> **I** must **not** contravene **the** School **Rules** and **Regulations** without **expecting** to **incur** the **appropriate** penalty **from** those **in** authority.

At a gathering in October 2002 of old pupils who had left in 1971 – the very last to be educated entirely in the Grammar School – it was amusing to find that though they had some difficulty remembering all the words of the School Song they were word-perfect when it came to rattling off the school line. I noticed, however, that by 1971 'contravene' had been replaced by 'disobey'.

Though the good order of the school in general was the responsibility of the Headmaster, the girls came under the eagle eye of Miss Sawdon, who for many years kept a strict control of their behaviour, appearance and even their deportment. Whereas the boys wore a fairly simple uniform, with easily-standardised blazers of maroon, edged with green braid (gold braid for prefects), the girls' uniform was more complicated and subject to aberrations such as fashionable petticoats or fancy stockings. They also wore blazers, but underneath, the junior girls wore a white blouse, with a tie and a kind of pinafore dress or gymslip. After the Second Year summer dresses were worn, with the alternative of green or maroon stripes. There were even regulation knickers of official King James's bottle green. I can record that there was at least one infringement of the knickers rule. One of the 1971 leavers recalled that he had seen a First Year girl dance on top of a desk – and she was wearing white!

An improved boys' cap was introduced in 1958, with a larger peak and a multi-coloured badge. The girls' equivalent was a green beret with badge, worn – at the correct angle – by all girls, who were regularly inspected. The perennial problem of how long the skirt should be was easily solved: each girl had to kneel down, and if the skirt then touched the floor, all round, it was deemed to be of a respectable length.

Not much point in wearing a smart uniform, though, if a girl moved around in an ungainly, slouching manner. So Miss Sawdon, Miss Chew and the PE staff also trained the girls to walk correctly – with feminine elegance, a book balanced on the head to encourage an erect bearing. One of the earliest payments from the School Fund (1956) is recorded as 'Deportment Badges £8.2.0d.'

The late 1950s and 1960s were, in general, one of the happiest periods in the life of the school. To counterbalance all the outward formality of smart uniform, firm discipline and the constant striving for good results in both games and exams, there was the lighter and livelier side provided by a wide range of societies and out-of-school activities. Most noteworthy of these were the dramatic productions, some involving as many as sixty staff and pupils. In addition to the one-act plays of the Inter-house Drama Competition, there was a series of full-length school plays of real quality directed by Molly Sawdon – *His Excellency, The Lady's not for Burning,* and most notably *Hamlet* (1959), in which the title-role was brilliantly played by Desmond Gill. Other characters who are still remembered include Ophelia (Davena Burn), Horatio (Rex Taylor) and Osric, played by Stuart Herrington who, only a few years later, returned to teach chemistry. The moving climax of *Hamlet* anticipated a real-life sorrow. Desmond Gill, the winner of the school's first scholarship to RADA, and with a fine career ahead as an actor, died at the early age of 52.

Building operations, to be described later, meant that drama was suspended until the autumn term of 1964, when Miss Sawdon directed a production of *Much Ado about Nothing* in the new School Hall. After this, productions were mainly by Mr M A Storr, who later became Head of English and Drama, serving the school from 1965 until 1993. The disruption caused by the builders had its effect on out-of-school activities as well as lessons, and it is a tribute to the staff and pupils of this time that so much good work was carried on.

Allied to drama was the Spoken English Competition, introduced by Mr Brewin in the summer term of 1956, and with the support of Miss Sawdon, a voluntary annual event. Prizes were now awarded each year for Senior Spoken English and Junior English Reading, adjudicated by an invited guest. The seniors, after reciting a poem, had to speak for five minutes on a topic of their own choice, usually producing entertaining items of a high standard. It is interesting to note, if we move ahead to 1967, that the prizewinner that year was Geoffrey Wilkinson, who had also won the Inter-house Drama competition for Nidd House by producing and acting in Ionesco's *The Bald Prima Donna.* He later became the famous actor of film and television, under the stage-name of Tom Wilkinson.

Further training in public speaking was provided by the Debating Society, revived in 1955 by Mr W P D Murphy, Head of History. The following year, as well as resurrecting the Gramophone Society, where we had our own Desert Island Discs, I formed the Junior Debating Society, and in 1958, when Bill Murphy left, I took over the running of the Senior Debating Society, and managed to keep it going until 1974. Chairing and guiding those lively after-school debates in the art room – sometimes for an hour or so with an attendance of as many as a hundred – was always a pleasure. It was easy enough to think of new topics, but finding proposers and seconders was a problem. So it became my custom to lie in ambush and button-hole potential speakers as they walked down the corridors – and I must say that some of those press-ganged, arm-twisted debaters turned out to be the very best.

Over the years a great variety of subjects was covered by the Debating Society, sometimes in joint meetings with Harrogate Grammar School, and also the Parents and Friends Association. Many of the things we discussed were the perennials still in fashion – euthanasia, nuclear weapons, the supernatural, smoking, immigration, pop idols, vivisection, marriage and 'This House would rather elect a President than support the Royal Family', heavily defeated, and (with Harrogate Grammar School) 'There is too much ado about Shakespeare' – easily carried. But others reflected topics of the day, the most significant of these being a talk, followed by discussion, given by Mr A A Ingham, the Divisional Education Officer. This was on the controversial new concept of 'Comprehensive Schools' – interestingly given at King James's as early as the 31st October 1958.

Other topics which show what was in fashion at the time were Mods and Rockers, the Flower Children, the Beatles and so on. Geoff Wilkinson, incidentally, easily won the motion that 'Speech Day is an Unnecessary Evil', though lost the motion (86 votes to 21) in 1967 'that beards are abominable' to Mr Ian Porter (biology), who sported a fine beard to make his case. Staff often came along to support the meetings, such as the time when Mr W J Clark of the French department blew cigarette smoke through his handkerchief in a convincing demonstration of the way lungs were stained by the habit under discussion. The staff also rallied to form panels for a number of popular sessions of 'Any Questions?'

Musical activities continued to thrive, with talented soloists like John Allan (violin) and Paul Mann (piano) who was also helping in the Gramophone Society, now using the school's new 3-speed record player. Much musical help was given by Mrs Kettlewood (1941-1964), who taught chemistry, a short and nimble lady who had mastered the double-bass. Mr Brewin, also a double-bass player and pianist, helped out in the small school orchestra, on one occasion conducting. Details of various concerts, many directed by Miss Rushforth, are given in the *Challoner*, which also records, in 1958, the founding of a Jazz Appreciation Society and a Madrigal Society, the latter by Mr Ian Day, himself a fine tenor. The following year, 1959, Mr Joe Bertram left, to be succeeded by Mr Tom Benstead. That year, too, 'Prof' Watson retired, and was replaced by Mr M Almond, whose name, along with eccentricity, provided the nickname of 'Nutty'. Under his direction, and that of his successors, Mrs Jenkins and Mr Cyril Dodd, both orchestra and choir were gradually built up, offering more ambitious programmes, including a production of Gluck's *Orpheus* in 1966, in which Linda Baxter, in the title-role, sang a memorable *'Che farò?'*, a foretaste of her later operatic career.

Some societies in that period had a large following – the Film Society, for example, started in October, 1957, by Mr Bryan (biology), with Mr Norman as projectionist, later run by Mr Watts, who had replaced Mr Murphy as Head of History, and Mr Briggs, who had replaced Mr Bryan as Head of Biology. Others attracted smaller numbers, but were greatly appreciated. In the 1950s and 60s there were clubs for Badminton, Tennis, Table Tennis, Hiking, Basketball, Gymnastics and Scottish Dancing, as well as the more sedentary Scripture Union, a Bridge Club run by Mr Wilson and Mr Kirkham, and the elite Chess Club, founded in 1956 at Mr Brewin's suggestion by Mr Beetham, and from 1963 run by his colleague, another first-class chess player, Mr Jowsey.

Before we leave this summary of out-of-school activities some mention should be made of the series of mock elections which we organised as an off-shoot of the Debating Society. The first was in the spring term of 1959. I remember that I was hesitant about approaching Mr Brewin, knowing how disruptive it would be if we did the job properly. He was, in fact, very supportive, giving us permission to run a full election campaign over a fortnight or so, with posters, banners and slogans all over the school, leaflets appearing on every desk, and five rival parties competing for attention in the playground every break and lunchtime, with plenty of heckling and clowning. In addition to the major political labels we had a comic party, the

The first of several mock elections (1959) organised by the author. Candidates, front row, from left: T Newell, Labour (68), D Simmons, Liberal (52), T Wood, Conservative (200), D Burn, Troglodyte (128), D Poskett, Communist (33). Timothy Wood was later elected real-life MP for Stevenage.

Troglodytes, who campaigned for staying indoors and just watching television. Ballot papers were provided by the obliging school secretary, Mrs Marjorie Rendle, not long before she was replaced the following year by Mrs Cohen. Voting took place from lunch-time onwards on the 4th May, with a gratifying 92% voluntary turn-out of the school. The result, announced by the Headmaster at morning assembly, was:

Burn, David (Troglodyte)	128
Newell, Timothy (Labour)	68
Poskett, David (Communist)	33
Simmons, David (Liberal)	52
Wood, Timothy (Conservative)	200

An interesting sequel was that Timothy Wood later became the real-life Conservative MP for Stevenage. Tim Newell later became Deputy Governor of Armley Jail, about the same time, in fact, that his sister, Janet Newell, became Deputy Head of King James's School.

The school's first mock election proved so popular that we decided to hold another in the summer term of 1963, the comic party this time being the Utopians. The result was as follows, the total number of voters being exactly the same as before:

Bedford, John Aubry (Conservative)	73
Hall, Eric Bruce (Utopian)	97
Hornsey, David John (Liberal)	121
Warhurst, David Edward (Labour)	132
Watson, John James (Social Democrat)	58

Winners of the Marshall Prize and Stevens Prize, about to leave Knaresborough Castle Girls' School for KJGS in 1961. From left: Heather Brearley, Carol Milner, Ann Kaminski, Susan Welch.

Letting off a little steam in this way did no harm to the exam results, which over those years were consistently good, and sometimes outstandingly good – an achievement which some attributed to the controversial introduction, soon after Mr Brewin's arrival, of 'the fast stream' in 1956, whereby selected A forms took their GCE O Level exams in four years rather than five. Occasionally there were really high-flyers, like that remarkably self-effacing boy, Roger Marshall, who in 1959 at the age of sixteen, won a State Scholarship, with distinctions in all his A Levels in maths, physics and chemistry. Around this time Open Scholarships were won by Rex Taylor (geography) and Tim Wood (maths), and the school received news of a first-class honours degree in English at Cambridge and a fellowship at Harvard won by John Rathmell, and first-class honours in biochemistry at Leeds by Ann Nicholson.

Yet the conditions in which good exam results were obtained were by no means ideal. The hall/gymnasium was now too small for exam sessions and there was a general problem of overcrowding. Small groups of Sixth Formers were being taught in the Headmaster's study, and even in the changing-rooms. By 1961 Mr Brewin was able to report a total of 583 pupils, 101 of whom were in the Sixth Form, but also that 'the extensions, so long dreamed of and discussed, have begun to take place'.

Temporary wooden classrooms had been provided by the West Riding Authority, the most recent in 1958. These were pleasant enough to teach in, but tended to be too cold in winter and too hot in summer, with noisy air conditioners. Now, for what today would seem the ridiculously small sum of £125,000, there would be not only better classrooms, but a new gym, woodwork room, library, a new science block and a large hall for assemblies, drama and concerts.

Most of this building work was done between 1961 and 1963 while the school was in session. What banging, hammering and clattering surrounded us as we tried to get on with our teaching! Neither staff nor pupils who worked through that trying period will ever forget the noise of the machines, the shouts of the workmen, the mountains of rubble, the mounds of sand and stacks of bricks, with noise and dust infiltrating everywhere. The workmen themselves could be a distraction – especially to the girls, who were assembled by Miss Sawdon and solemnly warned that on no account must they 'fraternise' with the workmen. Bad though conditions were, however, they were as nothing compared with the volcanic upheaval of the much bigger building operations soon to be started in anticipation of the new Comprehensive School.

At last, by the summer of 1963, after delays and set-backs, the dust had settled, the noise had ceased and the unsightly debris – along with the workmen – had vanished. The person most relieved to see the end of the alien occupation of his territory must have been the Caretaker, Albert Scurrah, who was then in his 35th year at King James's.

The showpiece was the 'New Hall', whose prefabricated roof of specially-designed acoustic ridges we had seen lowered into place by a gigantic crane. It was here that the whole

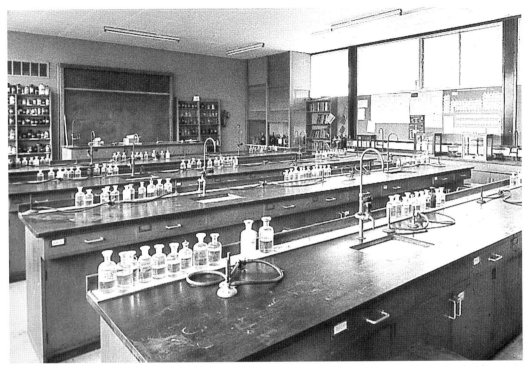

Chemistry laboratory in the new Science Block soon after its completion in 1963.

school assembled on the 7th May 1964 for Speech Day and, in the afternoon, for the official opening of the new buildings by the Rt Hon Lord James of Rusholme, Vice-Chancellor of the University of York, the gathering presided over by the Chairman of the Governors, Councillor Albert Holch.

After a plaque had been unveiled in the entrance hall, where four metallic murals (now in the Design Block) aroused much argument, the school orchestra and choir performed items from the reign of James I, and the National Anthem was sung. The school was then open until 9-30pm to enable guests, parents and friends to see displays by various departments – hands-on experiments in physics and chemistry, dissected frogs and rats in biology (presided over by Claude, the school skeleton), domestic science demonstrations, a gym display and an art exhibition. Conveniently adjacent to the entrance hall visitors could see the new school offices, including that of the Headmaster, moved from the old cramped quarters near the Headmaster's house.

The staff involved in games, principally Mr R M Hearld, who had taken over from Tom Benstead in 1963, and Miss J W Lewis, who had taken over from Miss S V Russell the previous year, were as much interested in developments outside the school as in the new buildings. There had been difficulties for both games and sports, these sometimes having been held on the field some distance away at Haya Park. But Sports Day had continued much as before, though now with the sad addition to the trophies of one presented in memory of a promising Sixth Former, Anne Coore, whose tragic death had taken place in 1963.

A long-awaited improvement was achieved in 1965, when the KJGS field at the bottom of Aspin Lane was exchanged for the one at the top which had belonged to the Knaresborough Cricket Club. Combined with the adjacent school field this would soon give a generously large green space, conveniently close, screened from Aspin Lane by newly-planted whitebeams. Though at first causing extra work, this re-ordering of the games and sports field was to the great advantage of our faithful Groundsman, Frank Bailes, who cycled to school every day from Starbeck. Frank, in his flat cap and with fresh-air cheeks, was to give the school nearly 33 years of service by the time of his retirement in 1974. Bob Hearld later paid tribute to him as a gentleman and a Christian, with a quaint old-fashioned style. He recalled a rugby match, in which bodies were flying everywhere, with Mr Bailes 'delicately wending his way through them, marking out the pitch'. Many will remember him maintaining those prominent white lines and riding round the sports fields on his new-fangled petrol mower.

Cross-country running has always been a strong tradition at the school. Here is Mr Bob Hearld, with the U16 team, Claro Area Champions in 1964.

By 1965, then, King James's Grammar School had good facilities, inside and out, and apparently everything going for it. But it was not to remain a compact, well-established little grammar school for long. Already there was talk of it expanding, combined with two other schools, to become a Comprehensive School at least three times its present size.

Under 13 Cricket (1965), with Mr Raymond Nudds. The Captain is Peter Winter. Sitting on his right is David Nudds; standing on his left is Harry Winter.

9. The Last Days of the Grammar School (1966-1971)

As a maths man, as well as a traditionalist, Mr Brewin must have relished the instinctive bit of arithmetic which confirmed that 1966 would be the 350th anniversary of the school's foundation. His decision to celebrate it in style followed nicely on the completion of the new buildings. The prospect of possible comprehensive transformation only intensified his determination to show that Dr Chaloner's school had both triumphed over many vicissitudes and had recently completed a particularly satisfactory phase in its contribution to the community. The Headmaster, in fact, was proud of his school, and whatever the future might bring, he wanted its history and heritage to be fully recognised.

The most important aspect of the 350th anniversary was the provision of proper Armorial Bearings, officially registered with the College of Heraldry. As previously mentioned, the school badge was simply based on the design of the seal used by the Knaresborough Urban District Council. Neither this nor the school's version of it had ever been registered as a coat-of-arms, and Mr Brewin rightly decided that, at least as far as King James's was concerned, the matter should be put right.

He soon discovered that the registration fee, including professional art-work, would be expensive, though the sum would seem very small today. So he sent out a letter in March 1965 to as many old pupils as he could trace, appealing for contributions. Some would be amused to see that he could not refrain from including a snippet of a maths lesson. The total needed, he said, £262.10.0., divided by the number to whom his letter was being sent (more than 1,300) would require from each of them a contribution of only five or six shillings. There was a good response – as there was to the other appeal in the letter for contributions to a retiring present for Maud Scurrah, Cook-in-charge since 1928.

Mr Brewin, having thoroughly investigated the various possibilities, came to the conclusion that the new badge should be clearly distinguishable from the unregistered town emblem, mainly because otherwise 'it suggests that we are under the jurisdiction of the Urban District Council'. In good time for the anniversary, with the help of Dr Tate of Leeds University and Mr Turner of Harrogate, a splendid new coat-of-arms and crest was proposed, described in the jargon of the College of Heraldry as follows:

> *Arms* Azure on a mount in base vert, a castle with two domed towers or, each with a pennon flying to the sinister argent; on a chief of gold two crowns gules.

In plain English this refers to a gold-coloured castle frontage (the barbican gate of Knaresborough Castle) on a green mound, with a blue background. The little flags on the towers are flying to the left. Above this symbol of Knaresborough are two red crowns representing the kingdoms of King James I of England, James VI of Scotland.

The crest above the shield is described in a similarly intriguing way:

> *Crest* On a wreath. . . a demi lion gules crowned or, grasping in the dexter forepaw a sprig of oak proper, fructed or; pendent from a chain around the lion's neck a closed book. . . garnished all gold.

This refers to the conventional wreath, surmounted by a lion from the arms of Richard Plantagenet, Lord of Knaresborough, youngest son of King John, who granted a charter to Knaresborough Priory in 1257. This was apparently thought appropriate by the heraldic authorities 'as a reminder of the early education in the town, begun perhaps by the monastery'. A lion rampant is also in the arms of Scotland and a further reminder of King James. The sprig of oak (from the original seal) refers to the Forest of Knaresborough, and the golden book is 'a reference to knowledge and education'. (But why a closed rather than an open book?) Underneath are the three opening words of the school motto in Latin.

This splendid coat-of-arms was copied and painted by Messrs Bedford and Broadbank onto an oak panel set up on the left-hand side of the new hall. This panel was made by Mr Metcalfe, Head of Woodwork, with another on each side, on which the first part of the school motto was inscribed by Mr Jenkinson, Head of Art. The high point of the 350th anniversary was to be the ceremonial unveiling of the coat-of-arms by a distinguished guest.

The likelihood that Mr Brewin would make the most of this special anniversary had been predicted by the strong sense of tradition he had already shown. Soon after his arrival he had arranged for the prizegiving to be observed as Founder's Day, choosing a date in October 1956, as being nearest to the day Dr Chaloner made his application to King James. Numbers meant that two separate prizegivings for juniors and seniors had to be arranged, both for this and the following year, on 4th October 1957, which the Head seems to have regarded as the first real Founder's Day, because he made a point of thanking the governors for their support for the function that had been revived 'after a lapse of more than 20 years'. He also thanked Mrs Beaumont for her hard work in dealing with all the prizes, a task at which she became an expert. She also became an expert in setting questions, many gleaned from fellow-teachers, in the Inter-house Quiz she regularly organised for the senior school after the exams.

The first Founder's Day on which the whole school was able to assemble had been held on the 3rd October 1958 in a huge marquee erected just across the road on Fysche Hall playing field. Because of heavy rain the ground was reduced to mud and puddles, and bales of straw were hurriedly laid down. The essential feature, as on all these early Founder's Days, was the reading of extracts from the Letters Patent by the Head Boy and Head Girl, solemnly reminding staff and pupils of the seventeenth-century origins. On this occasion the main speech and prizegiving was by the Right Reverend Dr Donald Coggan, Bishop of Bradford. The Head's notes show that the cost of hiring the marquee for that occasion was £45, less than that of the prizes, £57. 1961 is the marquee Founder's Day that many of us will best remember. On a mild October afternoon the Dean of Ripon, the Very Reverend F L Hughes, immediately captured the attention of the audience of well over 500 with his opening remark: 'You know, this place is absolutely *crawling* with insects. . . And I assure you I didn't bring any of them with me!'

Five years later, on the 7th October 1966, it must have been a source of immense satisfaction to Mr Brewin to see the whole school assembled in smart uniform, in the recently-completed School Hall, in the presence of the brand new coat-of-arms attesting to 350 years of history. At the special 350th anniversary Founder's Day service it was unveiled by the chief guest, the Right Honourable the Earl of Harewood – an ideal choice because of his family's connection with Goldsborough and their longstanding support of the school. In the audience were a number of old pupils, one from New Zealand and two pupils representing Dr Chaloner's School at Amersham. The least that can be said of this anniversary concentration on historical matters, incidentally, is that from now on the name of the school magazine would have its correct spelling as the *Chaloner.*

After the prizes had been presented the school choir performed Stanford's *Te Deum*, conducted by the Head of Music, Miss S E Bateman. After giving a short speech, Lord Harewood (who commented that 'only the most odious people like making speeches') went to the top of the newly-re-ordered games field to plant a commemorative Turkey oak. It must be recorded, as a tiny fragment of history, that the tree subsequently died, and was quietly replaced with another, marked by the original plaque.

The 350th anniversary was also celebrated by the school being open to parents and visitors on the Friday and Saturday. The most important of the displays was in the library, where

Assembly in the recently completed School Hall, 7th October 1966 at the beginning of the 350th anniversary Founder's Day.

Richard Watts and Margaret Hunt had set out material relevant to their commemorative book, soon to be published. Central place was given to the original school Charter, with its great seal and interesting cameo portrait of King James. There were also the school rules of 1616 in their quaint original, with various items and photographs from the early days.

At this open day there were interesting things to see and handle, set up in the physics lab by Mr Wilson and in the biology lab by Mr Briggs. In the art-room Mr Jenkinson put on a display of watercolours, charcoal sketches and calligraphy. Mr Jowsey displayed books concerning Latin, and also Russian, a subject he had recently introduced. In the French department we played tapes of folk songs and demonstrated our latest acquisition, a loop projector, showing a cartoon character called Monsieur Carré, an aid to oral work and composition. By way of contrast I assembled a display of the various French text-books and readers used in school over the past fifty years. Drama was represented by scenes from *A Midsummer Night's Dream, She Stoops to Conquer* and the one-act play *The Form* by N F Simpson, which featured Geoff Wilkinson in the main comedy role, all these directed by Mr Mike Storr.

The previous December he had also directed a highly successful production of *The Importance of Being Earnest*, with Robin Pauley as Algie and Linda Baxter as Lady Bracknell, later performed with riotous acclaim before the inmates of Thorp Arch open prison. Mike Storr followed this with other successes such as *The Crucible* (1967), with Martin Collins as a superb John Proctor, *The Government Inspector* (1968), *Romeo and Juliet* (1969), with Judith Symonds as the perfect Juliet, *A Night Out* (1970) and *The Fire Raisers* (1970) – all this in addition to the Inter-house Drama Competition.

The activity in drama serves to illustrate that in the late 1960s there was more to school life than extended premises and events connected with the 350th anniversary. Though cricket suffered because it was without a home ground while the new field was being prepared, games in general continued to be enjoyed, teams in football, hockey and tennis travelling to Harrogate, Ripon, York, Thirsk and Easingwold. Societies continued as before, including the Debating Society, with a third mock election – timed to anticipate the General Election – held

on the 28 March 1966. This time the comic party was 'Thrush', a reflection of the fact that everybody was then watching the television series *The Man from UNCLE*. The winners were the Conservatives, led by Martin Hampar, with Labour (Gregory Richardson) a close second, followed by the Liberals (Angus McDonald), Thrush (Bill Robinson) and the Radical Party (John Gandy).

A number of retirements and staff changes occurred around this time. After school on the 30 April 1965 a gathering of grateful consumers of school dinners met to say goodbye to Mrs Maud Scurrah. They included old pupils like David Warhurst, and also present from the early days here was Mrs Robinson. Councillor Holch and Miss Sawdon paid tribute, and as a token of our appreciation and affection, we presented Maud with a handbag and an armchair, in which, she assured us, Albert would never be allowed to sit. We were fortunate in having Mrs Collins to take over the important position of queen of the kitchen. Albert Scurrah, our Caretaker, retired a couple of years later than Maud, in September 1968, after completing 40 years at the school, like his better half. She must have kept her word about not letting him sit in her armchair. As his retirement present Albert chose an armchair of his own.

Albert and Maud, the uncrowned King and Queen of King James's Grammar School, both serving 40 years as Caretaker and Cook-in-charge respectively

Also in 1965 there retired two teachers who had each served here for over twenty years – Mrs E Ellis, who as Miss Lancaster had married Mr F F Ellis and had taught French and English, along with involvement in drama and the arranging of flower displays in school, and Mrs M Kettlewood, who taught chemistry and made such a useful contribution to both the choir and orchestra. The following year saw the departure of Miss Margaret Hunt (history) and Mrs Louise Turton (English), as well as Mr Cyril Dodd (music), replaced by Miss S E Bateman (who later became Mrs Millward).

In 1967 there were especially good exam results, with Alan Winter, for example, gaining four As at A Level, the ICI prize and a place at Cambridge in natural sciences. Staff changes included Bill Clark (French) leaving, to be replaced by Mrs Valerie Barnwell. In September 1967 Mr Maurice Armsby was appointed Head of Music. One of his first moves was to break with tradition – and get away with it! He discarded the music written for the school song by 'Prof' Watson and substituted a composition of his own, the school singing this for the first time on Speech Day 1968, since which date it has been the accepted tune. In 1968 another old pupil, Janet Malthouse, returned as a teacher, Mrs Coatman (geography), to join others like Mrs Chatten (from 1963) who had been here as Janice Apew and married a KJGS boy, Brian

Chatten. Miss T H Calvert became head of girls' PE in place of Miss Joanna Lewis, who later married Bob Hearld, Head of boys' PE.

Major staff changes in 1970 were, in addition to the departure of Mrs V J Smart (domestic science) the retirement of two great characters known to generations of pupils. First, Mr J B Jenkinson, better known as 'Joe Jenks', Head of Art for 25 years. His interest extended to pottery, weaving, wood-carving, fishing and rock-climbing, especially in the Lake District, to the fringe of which he retired, at Kirkby Stephen. Joe will be long remembered, not only for his own outstanding talent in drawing and painting, but for his quiet, droll manner and conversation sparkling with humour. I remember how, like many of us, he had a time-table stuck on the inside of the door of his staff-room locker. Only this one was different. It was blank except for a few crosses, which from time to time he would consult. These crosses, we soon discovered, indicated when the Headmaster was teaching – and unlikely to be patrolling the school. These were the periods when you would find Joe, with his mug of tea, entertaining us in the staff-room, teaching his class in the adjacent art-room by remote control. On one occasion Joe had to substitute for an absent teacher. To his dismay he found that the subject was RE, with no work set. So he dished out some paper and wrote on the blackboard: 'Draw a parson, riding a bike'.

Richard Beetham, like Joe, was a personality whom neither staff nor pupils would ever forget. He had been in charge of maths here for 18 years. Though he was a brilliant mathematician, both solving and setting problems for the *Times,* he was interested in almost every other subject, including French (he'd read all the novels of Balzac) and Russian. His fund of knowledge was extraordinary, particularly concerning the origin of words, phrases and fables, facts and figures. If you asked him something he didn't know, he would have the answer for you next day, having searched through the volumes that lined his Harrogate home from floor to ceiling, mostly acquired by combing through second-hand bookshops and Oxfam sales. He had a fund of funny stories, was a fluent and witty debater, but never suffered fools gladly – and his loud Burnley voice could often be heard electrifying both class-room and staff-room, when – red in the face – he was berating some poor soul who had failed to follow his flawless logic, sometimes making the wretch stand on a chair until he or she saw the point. A life-long bachelor, Dick Beetham had a smiling charm and an eye for the girls, being unfailingly helpful to the succession of *demoiselles* who came each year as our *assistantes*.

Much more could be said about staff who have given long service to the school, enriching it so much that when they leave, they seem irreplaceable. But others come along to make their own distinctive contribution. Mr Jenkinson was replaced by Mr P E Kearney as Head of Art and Design, and Mr Beetham was replaced by Mr M J Wilkins as Head of Maths – both of them to give the years of wholehearted service that would take them through the formative stages of the Comprehensive School and beyond.

At a recent reunion of pupils from the last years of the Grammar School many testified to the happy family atmosphere they enjoyed. Few in those days 'crept like snails unwillingly to school'. On the other hand, when one man was asked what his happiest memory of school life was, he replied: 'The last bell'. Some remembered the variety of physical punishments – not just the time-honoured rap with a ruler and styles of caning, but one master who brandished a cricket bat, and another a sawn-off billiard cue, though he used it essentially as a pointer for the blackboard.

An account of the life of a school could give the mistaken impression that it is parochial, too wrapped up in its own affairs. During this final period of the Grammar School there was a readiness to look outward. When Knaresborough was twinned with the German town of Bebra in 1969 the school was represented in the civic delegation to Bebra by a member

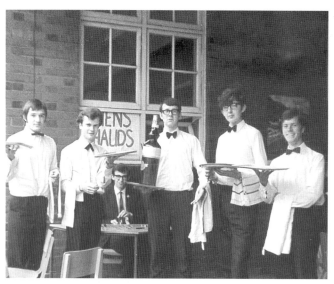

Garçon! Waiters at the school's second French Café (1966). The one with the huge bottle of wine is Geoff ('Tom') Wilkinson, later star of stage and screen. Next to him is John Bold, later Head of Architecture for the Royal Commission and Consultant on Cultural Heritage with the Council of Europe.

of the Sixth Form, Susan Foster. She was present, along with Councillor Holch and the Bürgermeister, Herr August-Wilhelm Mende, at the official twinning ceremony held in the Brüder-Grimm Schule, the school which would have strong links with King James's for years to come. In 1970 girls from the German school visited us, and a return visit was paid by two of our Sixth Formers, Angela Hoult and Susan Ramsden. It was Susan who made the very first pupil exchange in our town-twinning, becoming a friend of Dorle Wettlaufer, who has been back here in recent years.

Looking out into the wider world, the school raised money for many worthy causes, including work overseas. There were, for example, the activities of the Social Service Squad (eg visiting hospitals and providing Christmas hampers for local old people and 'the Borstal boys' at Wetherby) and support for Guide Dogs for the Blind (the favourite charity of Molly Sawdon and Paddy Wandsborough, who had taught PE here). Useful amounts were collected to help the hungry, particularly in Africa. In July 1966 we had organised our first French Café, partly to raise money for Oxfam, and also to create a French atmosphere. Tables with parasols were set out all along the front of the school, a red ribbon was cut by a young Frenchman, Bruno de Neuville, who gave an opening speech in French, then Sixth Formers, smartly and convincingly dressed, waited on at the tables, insisting that the orders were given only in French, all this to the authentic French sound of Mr Porter on his accordion. One of our visitors was Miss Alice Wood, formerly Head of French and Senior Mistress. The Café was so popular that a second one was arranged, raising more money for Oxfam. A whole Oxfam Week was, in addition, organised by Mr Storr, during which a contribution came from every form in the school, resulting in the sum of £100 being sent to buy two cows in Kenya.

The autumn of 1968 brought such grim television pictures of starvation in Biafra that we decided to organise a quick campaign for famine relief, encouraging volunteers to take a kind of bob-a-job card (an idea I'd found successful when running a Scout troop) on which volunteers recorded their money-raising activities. Others set up a coffee bar and disco, sold baked potatoes and hot dogs – and we offered the prize of a huge box of chocolates for the person (Mrs. Beaumont) who stuck a flag in the place on a desert island nearest the buried treasure. The total of £150 raised seems small today, but meant a lot then, especially in terms of altruistic involvement. Something even better, because it could be seen as anticipating the later link with the 'King James's School' in Sierra Leone, was started by Mr M A Lowe, Head of RE, in 1970. This was a society in support of Lepra, through which the school adopted four leper children in Africa, each costing £16 a year, with the prospect, at the end of two years, of a complete cure.

These are just a few examples of school activities which supplemented the work being carried on in classrooms, laboratories and on the games field. Outwardly school life went on as normal in the years leading up to 1971. But under the surface there was much unease and uncertainty amongst the staff about the changes that would be involved in the school becoming comprehensive. The burden of reorganisation, of planning, of estimating and calculating, and of all the extra meetings and paperwork, site visits with architects and so forth, fell mostly on the shoulders of the Head and senior staff, especially Molly Sawdon, who was the officially styled Senior Mistress and Deputy Head, as well as being in charge of the Sixth Form. Her contribution to the planning for the new school was considerable, and seems to have been made harmoniously, in spite of the forceful characters involved. Recalling how she had served with three very different Headmasters, she recently told me: 'I got on with them all'.

Mr Brewin cannot at first have been in the least enthusiastic about being offered the headship of a comprehensive school. His reservations could already be seen at the Governors' Meeting held on the 15th March, 1966, when the Divisional Education Officer, Mr. J V Rawcliffe, presented the 'Report and Recommendations of the Divisional Executive's Working Party' on the organisation of secondary education in the area. This was the key document, on which the governors were asked to submit their observations.

Whatever the governors thought, the decision was taken at county and national level to go ahead, and at the Governors' Meeting on 6th December that year they were handed a 'Statement of Justification to extend accommodation . . . to form an 8 Form entry 11-18 Comprehensive School.' Mr Brewin had invited the educationalist, Dr Kathleen Ollerenshaw, to be the speaker at the Founder's Day and prizegiving in 1968. By this time, comprehensivisation, as in most parts of the country, was inevitable, having been finally approved for Knaresborough by the Department of Education and Science on he 27th February 1968 – and Dr Ollerenshaw was glad to point out in her speech that 'the best way to go comprehensive was to base the new school on an existing grammar school, especially one with long-standing traditions, such as King James's Grammar School'.

This was the view Mr Brewin now came to terms with, eventually working with commendable vigour on the reorganisation which was the only option. It was noticeable that, as usual, he did not like to delegate, but took on most of the prodigious task himself. The staff were naturally apprehensive about their future – with the obvious exception of those about to take what they saw as a well-timed retirement. These included Mrs Mary Wilson (née Dixon), retiring after 33 years, and Mr John Metcalfe, after 32 years. An article in the school magazine, 'Two Quiet Lives', paid tribute to their long and loyal service, Mary in games and school trips, as well as teaching languages, 'Johnnie' as the school's First Aid man, as well as teaching woodwork and RE. He will also be remembered for his craftsmanship in the table, lectern and other items he provided for the School Hall.

As details of the new arrangements became known, and especially in cases where there would be an increase in salary, status or facilities, teachers became more optimistic. Heads of departments, for example, were expecting an increase in the amount allocated for their requisitions of books and equipment. It would mean for most of us, a major upheaval, but it could also be seen as a stimulating challenge, something to bring the best out of us.

There was nothing stimulating about the first tangible evidence of the Comprehensive School – the start of work on the new buildings. Scheduled to open in the September term of 1971 the building operations started soon after plans were finalised in 1968. So this meant at least a couple of years of disruption, all the more intolerable for many of the staff who had

King James's Grammar School in its final term, June 1971.

The last staff to serve at King James's Grammar School, June 1971. Front, from left: H Horseman, T J Sayles, M Winter, J R Metcalfe, B M Sawdon, F Brewin, C S Walker, N Beaumont, W H Jowsey, P R Nudds, A Kellett. Middle: W Sleight, J Collins, M Grint, V A Cohen, J M Couzens, J Chatten, M Sayles, T H Calvert, V J Barnwell, J Coatman, M R Rowley, P Fulcher, F Bailes. Back: M Armsby, R F Watts, S J Herrington, M A Storr, J Wilson, R M Hearld, P E Kearney A L Kirkham, D A Briggs, M A Lowe, M J Wilkins.

been obliged to teach through the chaos of construction only about three years earlier. The way both teachers and their classes soldiered on in these inimical conditions deserves to be noted and applauded.

It so happens that I have good documentary evidence, on old super 8 mm colour film, of just how disruptive the building work was. One of the reasons I had set up the French Café was to make short films for the loop projector of French scenes useful for teaching the O Level six-picture French composition. One, for example, involved a very willing young actor called Duce, a lad with an enormous appetite, who ordered and consumed mounds of French food – then found he had no money to pay for it, and was forced to *faire la vaisselle*. Another concerned a burglar who stole the school cups. (In later life he ended up as one of several psychiatrists produced by King James's.) Some of the other scenes we filmed were near the building sites, and this is why I ended up making a documentary covering the last days of the Grammar School and the establishing of the new Comprehensive.

The film contains shots of buildings coming down, but mostly of others going up. As it is silent, though, it can give no idea of the distracting cacophony of bull-dozers, pneumatic drills, cement mixers, and all the shouting, swearing, singing and loud radios of the workmen. The row ceased for a while in March 1970, when the firm of contractors were silenced by bankruptcy, and other builders had to be found. There was also less noise as the work neared completion, and fortunately some of the biggest jobs, especially the great Sports Hall, were situated well away from the main school.

We experienced no winding down in the social life during this last year of the Grammar School. There was the drama and music already referred to – with a particularly fine

Christmas concert, and James Potter as a member of the National Youth Orchestra, later to become principal cellist with the Royal Ballet. There were well-fought games and flourishing societies – and a most enjoyable trip to Annecy and Paris, led by Mrs Barnwell, Mrs Carpenter and myself.

By the summer term of 1971 the new school buildings had taken shape and the finishing touches were mostly to be applied to the interior. Mr Brewin, always conscious of the value of a historical record, arranged for two professional photographs to be taken – one of the staff of King James's Grammar School, including the Caretaker, Bill Sleight, and the Groundsman, Frank Bailes, and a panoramic view of all of the staff and children assembled on the playing field.

The contrast between the complex of new buildings, stretching down the hill towards the playing fields, and the small King James's Grammar School at the top, was remarkable. Here are a few samples of estimated expenditure for the last year of the life of KJGS (1970-71) to illustrate the small scale of things in the old school:

Salaries of all teaching staff	£56,145
Wages of other staff	5,155
Gas	275
Electricity	1,500
Cleaning materials	175
Water	80
Rates	2,030
Books	855
Library books	190
Apparatus and equipment	260
Examination fees	1,050

Expenditure from now on would be on a vast scale compared to this. And as we looked out from the old school to the pristine, untouched, unsoiled accommodation of the new, we appreciated that much of the provision was adequate and even generous. There would be snags as well as benefits, of course. Swings and roundabouts. But as we now counted the last numbered days of the Grammar School, we felt no sense of decline and fall. We had kept going to the end, and now looked forward to carrying something of this spirit into the new school, helping to justify its name – no mere 'Knaresborough Comprehensive', but 'King James's School'.

10. King James's School: The Settling-In (1971-1975)

King James's School, Knaresborough's brand-new comprehensive, opened on Tuesday, the 7th September 1971, anticipating by more than a term its official opening in the February of 1972. The school started almost a week later than intended, with the builders' equipment still around and much to be finished, but sufficiently ready to make a start realistic.

In a sense, it was an expansion of the existing school, and officially still states in its letterhead, below the coloured coat-of-arms:

Incorporating King James's Grammar School
Founded 1616

But it is simplistic to think of it as King James's Grammar School which 'went comprehensive'. It is true that this was by far the biggest and oldest of the three combining schools and that it was continuing on the same site. But this was, in fact, a complete re-organisation formed by the coming together, on equal terms, of Knaresborough Grammar School, the Knaresborough County Secondary Modern School and the Boroughbridge County Secondary Modern School.

The staff and children of Knaresborough Secondary Modern School had moved to King James's from their school buildings on Stockwell Road, leaving it vacant for occupation by Castle Church of England Primary School. The roots of Knaresborough Secondary Modern School could be said to be in the pioneering educational work of the Knaresborough Wesleyan Methodists, who ran the 'Sabbath and Day School', mentioned in an earlier chapter, holding it in the 1815 Chapel, just off the top of Gracious Street.

When a bigger, more ornate chapel was built on land adjacent to it in 1868, largely through the generosity of Isaac Holden, who had recently become Liberal MP for Knaresborough, the older chapel was adapted for use as a school, with an assembly hall and classrooms. Whereas the big Victorian chapel has been pulled down and replaced by a smaller Methodist Church (1975), the original 1815 chapel is still standing. It looks much the same as it always did on the outside, including the unusual flight of stone steps added at the back, worn hollow by thousands of little feet.

This building, known to earlier generations as 'the Waterloo Chapel', because it had been constructed in spite of many difficulties in the year of that famous battle, became the most important school for secondary education in the town, after the Grammar School. Records and figures are by no means complete, but in most of the Victorian period the attendance each Sunday morning and afternoon was never less than a couple of hundred, and there were about half this number attending the day-school during the week. The Education Act of 1870, which required elementary schools to be provided where voluntary education was not adequate, led the Knaresborough Improvement Commissioners to carry out a survey in which it was found that the Wesleyan Methodists had 230 places for children, presumably all in the 1815 schoolroom – and by 1878 a surviving register shows that the Methodists were teaching 287 children.

By 1895, as well as the two National Church of England Schools in Castle Yard and the Roman Catholic School in Church Lane, the *Knaresborough Almanack* was listing the 'Wesleyan School, Chapel Street,' with the Headmaster as Mr Knapton. In 1907 this Wesleyan school was taken over by the West Riding County Council, who took a lease on the premises, but also began to think about building a new secondary school for Knaresborough in Stockwell Road.

The excellent new buildings there had taken shape, in spite of wartime difficulties, by 1915. And, even before the work had been completed, the education authorities ordered a hasty transfer from the old 1815 building to this new one, built exactly a century later, moving everything, lock, stock and barrel, using children to carry some of the items down to Stockwell Road. This haste reflected an anxiety to prevent the new building from being requisitioned by the army – something which then happened to the 1815 Chapel as soon as it was vacated, a move which was repeated during the Second War.

The Headmaster at the time was Mr Samuel Carter, a lively, jovial character, who was a good conversationalist, as well as an effective disciplinarian. Sam Carter was to be remembered in Knaresborough for his forthright views and an intolerance of bureaucracy and form-filling. He would, for example, glance through the latest batch of papers requiring attention, tear them up and throw them into his waste-paper basket with the comment: 'They know all that already!. . . I'm a teacher, not a form-filler.' He had high standards for his pupils, including the least able, and used to claim – something which was unusual for those days – 'No child leaves this school without being able to read and write'. There was at the time an Infants department, with Miss Lonsdale in charge. Sam Carter would visit these younger children every week, hear them read – and then take out any who were not up to standard and give them about twenty minutes of extra coaching each week.

This was the man who presided over the move from 'Knaresborough Provided School' as it was then officially called, in the old chapel to the fine new 'Council School' in Stockwell Road. Sam Carter continued to give yeoman service to the school and the community until he retired in 1935. The next Headmaster was Jack Thompson, who also gave long service to the school, taking it successfully through the difficult years of the Second World War. He inherited buildings that had recently been extended and modernised, including new kitchens and excellent facilities for woodwork and metalwork. When metal was in short supply during the years of the Second World War he arranged for time spent in metalwork to be given to the 'Dig for Victory' campaign as pupils grew crops on land at Holly Bank. They also looked after animals – in particular, Larry the lamb and Wendy the goat.

Those who were at school under the headmastership of Jack Thompson, such as Fred Healey, described him as 'firm but fair' – something which would also be said of the longest-serving of the teachers at the Knaresborough Secondary Modern School, Mr Arthur Prest, always known as 'Wiggy' Prest, because he had lost all his hair in a childhood illness. He started teaching here in 1925, insisting on pupils giving their best in both spoken and written English, and had a particular interest in encouraging a love of poetry – the latter so successful that recordings of his pupils were made by the BBC. Arthur Prest, for many years Deputy Head, retired in 1964, after making a remarkable contribution over his 39 years here to the cultural life of the school. He produced many plays such as *The Black Tulip, Storm Island* and *Campbell of Kilmohr,* and was involved in the annual Festival of Music and Dance, which included a verse-speaking competition. From 1950 there was a particularly good contribution from the new Head of Music, Mr Phil Brown, notable for his popular productions of Gilbert and Sullivan, with an augmented orchestra, but sung entirely by pupils.

Jack Thompson left in 1956 to take up a post as organiser of Further Education, and was replaced as Headmaster by Mr Lance Crosby, who had come from Starbeck Secondary School. The Senior Mistress at this time was Miss Doris M Hamilton, a strict disciplinarian. She had replaced, in 1955, Miss Dorothy A Arnold, who was a teacher of art and needlework, as well as Senior Mistress, and had given the school 35 years of service. In his short time there (three years) Mr Crosby saw the numbers increase to around 450 and was able to make use of additional premises at Chain Lane, where there were modern facilities for metalwork, domestic science and also a laboratory for rural science.

The emphasis on rural science – later to find an important place in the Comprehensive School – was encouraged by the next Headmaster, Mr Arthur Lancefield, appointed in 1959.

The large gardens at Chain Lane and Stockwell Lane were put to good use, the latter site including sties where pigs were bred and chicken-runs where poultry was reared, the ducks having been hatched in incubators in the science lab.

There were, of course, many outdoor pursuits, including games and athletics, and participation in the Lyke Wake Walk. But academic subjects were not neglected. Mr Lancefield added French to the curriculum and arranged for more able pupils to take a 13+ test leading to transfer to a technical school. A small number had been transferred to King James's School, with great success, and under Mr Lancefield a larger number went to Harrogate High School when Mr Kimber was Headmaster. There was also close liaison with Harrogate College of Further Education under Mr Drake, to which many pupils transferred at the age of 15. In 1966 the first group of a dozen pupils stayed on for a fifth year to take the new CSE exam. There were some excellent results, several of the group going on to top jobs in teaching, the army and industry. Mr Michael Brass, who had replaced Arthur Prest as Head of English, did not move to the new Comprehensive School, but a strong team of teachers from Knaresborough Secondary Modern School did

Mr Arthur Lancefield, Headmaster of Knaresborough County Secondary School (1959-71), after which he was the first Deputy Headmaster of King James's School.

Mr R C Simpson, Deputy Head of Knaresborough County Secondary School, with the first candidates to take the new CSE exam in 1966. Mr Simpson ('Sinbad') continued to teach maths at King James's School, as well as being a Group Teacher.

so, including Miss Betty Crowther (Senior Mistress and art), Mr R C Simpson (Senior Master and maths), Mr K B Hirst (science), Mr H J Fountain (Science), Mr J Mawdsley (history), Mr P A Brown (music), Mr R J Burnett, (art), Mr Sid Ibbotson (woodwork), Mr. B J Warnes (crafts), Mrs L Henderson (domestic science), Mr J D Weatherill (P E) and Miss M C Foster (RE).

The third component of the Comprehensive School was Boroughbridge Secondary Modern School. This had its origins in a Church of England school serving Boroughbridge, Aldborough and surrounding villages, which had been built in 1854, replacing earlier nineteenth-century schools in St James's Square and New Row. In 1925 the Board of Education of the West Riding County Council inspected the school and decided that it was unfit for continued recognition until buildings and facilities had been put in order. From the 4th May 1926 it was taken over as a Council School and essential repairs and alterations started, the ultimate aim being to build a new school for an estimated 170 children, from seniors to infants.

By 1928 land had been bought from Lady Lawson-Tancred, and the new school – hailed as one of the most modern in the North of England – was opened in September 1932 at a cost of £11,950. The opening ceremony was performed by Sir Percy Jackson, Chairman of the West Riding Education Committee, in the presence of many distinguished guests and the Headmaster of the senior school, Mr H W Frape, and the junior school, Mr A L Mawer.

The new school, built round a large grass quadrangle, impressed the guests by its pleasant setting and ample facilities, which included the fairly recent novelty of electric lighting and central heating. There were modern classrooms, an assembly hall, staff-rooms, cloakrooms and a woodwork and metalwork room with a forge. The man who presided over the woodwork from the second year of this new school (1933) right through until he moved to King James's School in 1971, was Jack Varley, for many years also Deputy Head. He described it as a happy country school, and had worked under all the Heads at Boroughbridge – Messrs Frape, Leadbetter, Spencer, Rutherford, Frank Hodgson (previously referred to) and Frank Andrews, the New Zealander who was to become Head of the Lower School at King James's.

Ken Gregson later recalled the same happy atmosphere of a small country school, efficiently but personally run by Mr Andrews, who held a formal staff-meeting only once a year, apologising for the inconvenience and treating everybody to strawberries and cream! Also making the move from Boroughbridge to King James's School were Vera Hunter (English), Ann Mettam (science), Nan Purvis (history), Sheila Ward (domestic science), Bob Gibbs (maths), Ken Gregson (rural science) and David Baccus (art).

When the three schools came together on that first exciting morning of the 7th September 1971 there was no way of telling which children

Mr Frank A Andrews (left) soon after his appointment as Headmaster of Boroughbridge County Secondary School in 1958, with Deputy Head, Jack Varley, teacher of woodwork since 1933.

had belonged to which school, except that they were, of course, identified by their friends and former teachers. Every child looked exactly the same, in so far as they were all wearing the new King James's uniform, designed and introduced by Molly Sawdon.

Emphasising the link with the King who was the Scottish James Stuart, the girls now wore one of three kinds of tartan kilts, with their differing background colour:

Lower School:	Royal Stuart tartan (red)
Middle School:	Hunting Stuart tartan (green)
Sixth Form:	Dress Stuart tartan (white)

The Lower School boys wore a tie of Royal Stuart tartan with their white shirt and green blazer, all the blazers carrying a prominent reminder of the school coat-of-arms on the left breast pocket.

As I recall that first day, I have an impression of all those children in their smart new uniforms wandering about in some sort of awe at the sheer size of the place. The school now extended from the entrance hall, left into the block that had formed the bulk of the Grammar School, and also straight forward along a corridor. To the right of this was the School Hall (also called S1) and straight ahead the new staff-room, a spacious area of mock-leather seating, overlooking a large quad and the Lower School, with three adjoining quiet rooms and a small kitchen. This was on the first floor of the Middle School block containing classrooms used mainly for history, geography and maths.

Down a flight of stairs you came, on the right, to the modern languages department, with a Sixth Form teaching-room and small staff-room. This bottom corridor always seemed narrow and was often crowded. I understand that the school had been given the choice of having wider corridors, but this would have been at the expense of classroom size. In the other direction the way led through a cloakroom and toilet area past other classrooms to the Lower School hall and dining-room. In separate blocks, at a lower level, were the departments of art, design and technology, the music block, with its own practice rooms, two new gyms with changing-rooms (one in lieu of a swimming pool, rejected because the town was campaigning for a pool of its own) and the showpiece of the development, a huge Sports Hall, which could more or less accommodate the whole school. Other changes were common-rooms for the Fifth as well as the Sixth Forms and a new cafeteria system for school dinners, which could now be had for as little as 12 pence.

One of the first things the staff noticed was that, in contrast to the short distances walked around our old schools, we now had to cover what seemed like several miles a week to reach some of our classes – not just on the level, but up and down the stairs and steps. No wonder the kids were bewildered on that first day. One little lad I remember passing my room (M8) again and again. 'What are you doing?' I asked him. 'Walkin', sir'. 'What do you mean?'. 'I'm just walkin'. . . . That feller down there told me to keep on walkin''

It would have helped matters if the time-table had been in apple-pie order, but there were gaps, clashes and anomalies, and it took a while before it was all sorted out. What was so much appreciated by the staff was that, though we came from three very different schools, we teachers all got on together so well. I do not remember any kind of awkwardness or disagreement in those first crucial days and weeks. There was, in fact, a pleasure in meeting the various personalities from the other schools – Dick Simpson, for example, from the Knaresborough Secondary Modern School, rather like a CID man, an expert in bringing to book the most wily culprits, and with the important job of Fire Prevention Officer – or Vera Hunter of Boroughbridge Secondary School, a wit and comic who had a wonderful way with the difficult kids. Choice snatches of humorous comment, bandied about amongst the staff, was one of the things that kept us going through all the stress of life in a big school.

This process of getting to know each other was an important part of pulling closer together in the common task of making the new school work. The biggest change was in the main staff-room, especially during break and lunch-time. In the old schools each staff-room was a small, rather cosy meeting-place, where you could relax and have a conversation about anything other than school, if you wished. Now it was all talking shop – earnest discussions of sets and lists and individual children. Everybody seemed to be going round with a sheet or two of paper, a register or mark-book. Eventually there would no end of things to be filled in, ranging from Merit Cards to Underperformance Lists. With the far greater numbers and complexities of the Comprehensive School there was a proliferation of paper-work and the ever-present probings of the fussy fingers of bureaucracy.

For the record, here is a full list of members of the valiant pedagogic army who toiled away to establish the new school in the early 1970s:

Headmaster	Mr F Brewin
Deputy Head	Mr A G Lancefield
Senior Mistress	Miss B M Sawdon
Head of Middle School	Mr C S Walker
Head of Lower School	Mr F A Andrews

Heads of department:

English	Mr M A Storr
Maths	Mr M J Wilkins
Modern Languages	Mr A Kellett
Science	Mr J Wilson
Art and Design	Mr P E Kearney
Chemistry	Mr J S Herrington
Physics	Mr A L Kirkham
Biology	Mr D A Briggs
Geography	Mr T J Sayles
History	Mr R F Watts
Classics and Russian	Mr W H Jowsey
General Studies	Mrs N M Beaumont
Housecraft	Mrs R M Young
Music	Mr M Armsby
PE (Boys)	Mr R M Hearld
PE (Girls)	Miss T H Calvert
Religious Studies	Mr M A Lowe
Rural Studies	Mr K W Gregson
General Science	Mr K B Hirst
Woodwork	Mr J W Varley
Metalwork	Mr R Littlefair
Remedial Department	Miss A Oldman

Other staff, mainly consisting of teachers from the three schools, but with a number of additional appointments, were:

Mr D D Baccus	Mr D J Crosthwaite
Mrs V J Barnwell	Miss B Crowther
Mr P A Brown	Mrs M Dobson
Mr R J Burnett	Miss M C Foster
Mr R A Charlesworth	Mr H J Fountain
Mr D Clayton	Miss W P Fraser
Mrs J Coatman	Miss C A Garner

Miss R Cox	Mr P R Nudds
Mr R Gibbs	Mrs N Purvis
Mr H Greenway	Miss M A Seager
Mrs M Grint	Mrs M Simmonds
Mr A Hemsworth	Mr R C Simpson
Mrs L Henderson	Mr F L Varley
Miss J A Holmes	Mrs S M Ward
Miss M Hughes	Mr B J Warnes
Miss A V Hunter	Mr J P Watts
Miss M E Johnson	Mr J D Weatherill
Mr M T Jones	Mr J B Webster
Mr J Mawdsley	Mrs M Winter
Miss A Mettam	Mrs R M Young

Part-time staff in the early years included: Mrs J Chatten, Mrs J Clark, Mrs W M Harrison, Mr Harry Horseman (retired in 1972), Mrs J Jarvis, Mrs J G Norledge, Mrs M Rowley, Mrs M Sayles, Mrs M F Swallow.

Nor should we forget the long succession of French, and later German, assistants who served us so well in conducting conversation classes in their respective languages.

Office staff at the three separate schools had never been large, usually with one Secretary and one or two assistants. The new organisation was not only far bigger, but required additional administrative work, with a busy staff led by Mrs Vera A Cohen, the Headmaster's Secretary, and including Mrs M Hudson (a former pupil), Mrs D Hurst, Mrs M Slights and later Mrs R Westmoreland. In the days devoid of photocopiers and printers we recall that duplication, especially for exams, based on stencils, made constant demands on the office staff.

No less busy, especially in those early terms, was the Matron, Mrs M Hamilton, the location of whose medical room could sometimes be found by following trails of trickling blood, from nose-bleeds or accidents, along the bottom corridor of M Block. The Groundsman, Frank Bailes, was mostly well away from the buildings teeming with lively youngsters, but the man who felt the pressure of all their youthful energy, often resulting in damage, was the Caretaker, who had replaced Albert Scurrah in 1968, Bill Sleight. He now lived in a house next to the school, but his principal store-room was not far from Matron's room – both centres for patching up, administering first aid to bodies and furniture. All the sturdy individual wooden desks had by now been replaced by tables – more prone to damage, but at least not covered underneath by sordid blobs of chewing-gum on the scale found everywhere today.

Discipline in the early days of King James's School was not the major problem some had feared. The greater numbers naturally meant that it was often harder work to keep order – and some of us remember as a particular trial those after-school 'bus duties', when we had to shepherd the queues waiting to be transported to the villages. The staff fortunately included a fair proportion of teachers with long experience and all the tricks of the trade when it came to handling restless and recalcitrant children. Such teachers had good control in their classrooms, which was evident as you walked passed and glanced through the window in the door. It was not uncommon to see everybody paying attention, some even sitting up as still as any waxworks. But these old hands also helped with the general discipline by using their instinctive authority as they walked about the school, especially in those corridors and stair-wells, so busy at every lesson-change. Whether they were children you taught or not, it was second nature to shout at anybody you spotted misbehaving, to stop any running, pushing, litter-dropping – and especially any fighting or bullying. True, there were a few hostile and disruptive children, with a certain amount of vandalism, but the vast majority were a pleasure to teach and – like the staff – keen to make the new school a success.

The most dramatic incident concerning behaviour took place a year or two after the school had settled down to generally good order and discipline. It was a romantic outburst of the kind you might associate with an Italian opera plot. . . Imagine the sensational news going round the school one lunch-time that, just over there, under 'the bridge' linking the top school buildings, a senior boy had stabbed his girl-friend. He had then walked straight down to the railway viaduct and jumped from the top into the Nidd. . . Fortunately, both he and the girl survived, and what could have been a tragic episode in the history of the school was handled with great sensitivity and delicacy by Miss Sawdon and Matron.

Romantic attachments were not uncommon, as in all mixed schools (and not just amongst the pupils!). Some, indeed, had the potential of lasting a life-time. It is said that marriages are made in heaven. Certainly, a considerable number have been made at King James's.

It is relevant to add at this point that many who had been educated at King James's were only too pleased to send their children here – and even see their grandchildren carrying on the tradition. It was so common to be told: 'Sir, you taught my Mum.' This could be seen as a sign of confidence in the school – and certainly was when, year after year, the pupils included a significant proportion of children whose parents were teaching in the same school.

In those early years what bothered many of us on the staff, especially the heads of department, was not discipline, but this bureaucratic bumf already referred to – an inevitable concomitant, apparently, of all large organisations. The sheets of paper seemed to multiply, filling our pigeon-holes in the staff-room, day after day, with notes and lists, especially about sets. Arranging the children into sets of roughly equal ability – common to certain groups of subjects – proved to be one of our biggest administrative headaches. It would have been so much easier to have put everybody into mixed-ability classes – something which many parents had expected – and feared – would happen. But, like most comprehensives, we found it more practical to teach sets in which, in theory, nobody would be disadvantaged by being left behind or bored by being too far ahead. It meant long meetings after school in anticipation of each term, and with discussion of individual adjustments as the need arose.

Much of this settling-in process and new administrative work had already taken place by the time the school had its official opening on the morning of Tuesday the 29th February 1972. As our opener we could, I am sure, have had no more appropriate and popular person than Her Royal Highness, the Duchess of Kent. My old movie film shows her arrival – charming, elegant and always at ease – in the company of the Lord Lieutenant of the West Riding. She was welcomed by Mr Brewin and Councillor Albert Holch, Chairman of the Governors, senior staff and civic guests. The Duchess had coffee with senior pupils in the library, was then taken on a tour of the school by Mr Brewin, presented with a bouquet by Fiona Welch, a brass ornament made by Ralph Armsby and shown the Charter and Grant of Arms by Mr Watts. Following the welcome ceremony in the school, the Duchess unveiled a bronze plaque and signed the visitors' book. On leaving she decided to do a short walkabout before getting into the car, to the delight of children assembled at the front of the school.

A town event was now being planned which would provide an unexpected opportunity for staff and pupils of the new school to work closely together. This was the Historical Pageant, conceived as part of the Knaresborough's celebration of the 600th anniversary of the Castle and Honour of Knaresborough becoming part of the Duchy of Lancaster under John of Gaunt. The Pageant, held in June and September 1972, was produced by Ron Burnett, art teacher and man of many parts. I wrote the script and stood on the battlements of the Castle, which we used as our stage, conjuring forth, as narrator, a fascinating range of characters from

HRH the Duchess of Kent at the official opening of King James's School, 29th February 1972 signing the visitors' book, with Chairman of Governors, Councillor Albert Holch.

HRH the Duchess of Kent at the official opening, receiving a bouquet from Fiona Welch, watched by Mr Andrews, Head of Lower School, with Mr Brewin (left) and the Lord Lieutenant.

Knaresborough's history. Mostly played by staff and children from the school, we had Ancient Britons, Romans, Angles (all blond) and Normans – Serlo de Burgh (Alan Hemsworth) being interviewed in French. Several actors and helpers came from the town, but most were from King James's, including pupils such as Andrew Watts (medieval music), Judith Symonds (Queen Philippa) and Larry Privett (demon and explosives expert), and staff such as Richard Littlefair (centurion), Mike Lowe (D'Estotville), Mike Wilkins (King John), Dave Crosthwaite (Brian de L'Isle), Keith Hirst (marauding Scot), Mike Storr (Richard II), Richard Watts (Cromwell), Jim Watts (Rev Thomas Collins) and Phil Brown (Blind Jack) – all showing the school both as valuing heritage and making a lively contribution to the community. The great success of the Pageant provided the inspiration, 28 years later, for our Knaresborough Millennium Pageant – again, with important participation from the school.

During the first year of the new King James's parents and staff were beginning to wonder how academic work was being affected by all the changes. Groups already preparing to take O and A Level exams at the end of the school year (to be sat for and invigilated in the new boys' gym, as well as in S1) had carried on much as they had in the Grammar School, though now often in different rooms and in the busier context of the Comprehensive School. There were more distractions, of course, and teachers were preoccupied with their own problems of re-adjustment. Yet there is no evidence that exam results suffered. On the contrary, Mr Brewin was only too pleased to record that at the end of the first year as a Comprehensive School we had achieved outstanding results, with 305 passes at O Level, 161 at A Level and the biggest number of university and college entrants (52) in the history of the school. These splendid results were shown in the programme of the 1972 Founder's Day, chaired by Dr Stanley Hazel, Vice-Chairman of the Governors.

Though credit must go to teachers and examinees for doing so well in such difficult times, this result, after all, was to some extent the product of the pre-existing system, and everybody was now looking to see whether this standard would be maintained and exceeded. There was no reason why it should not. The new King James's School had the double advantage of being surrounded by a well-favoured catchment area, and one which was also very attractive to those looking for teaching-posts. It had consequently started life with few of the problems that might beset a comprehensive in an inner city or some other difficult environment.

Over the years the school has naturally had its share of parents who have been critical or uncooperative, but in general relations have been excellent, including at the meetings when parents have been able to meet the teachers to discuss the progress of their children. Though the staff jokingly referred to these evenings as 'Staff versus Parents' they served as a useful addition to our written reports.

The non-academic side of school life had passed through its own times of adjustment. Mr Hearld, for example, recalls teething troubles such as the failure of the new 'all weather pitch' to live up to its name, and getting the pupils from the Boroughbridge school used to formal PE kit and compulsory showers. On the other hand, he rejoiced in new facilities, indoors and out, which led to a great improvement in standards and participation, with as many as a dozen teams representing the school at weekends. Eventually the school had its own bus, essentially to transport teams, affectionately known as '007', driven by Messrs Hearld and Weatherill.

The department was seen to be in a healthy state on the first Sports Day of the new King James's, held on Wednesday the 5th July 1972. It was on a far bigger scale than the school had ever known, taking the whole day. The 26 field events were held before break, and the 55 track events extended into the afternoon, with the climax of the tug-of-war final and the presentation of 21 cups, shields and trophies by Mr Peter Kendrew, a former Olympic swimmer. The four houses of the old KJGS had now been increased to six, names of distinguished local families having been added to two topographical ones. The points scored at the end of Sports Day, 1972, will also serve to indicate the new house names:

1st.	Harewood	311
2nd	Roundell	264
3rd.	Newby	259½
4th.	Crag	204
5th.	Forest	199½
6th	Slingsby	185

These names had been sensitively chosen – two from KJGS (Crag and Forest), two from Knaresborough Secondary Modern School (Roundell and Slingsby) and two from Boroughbridge Secondary Modern School (Harewood and Newby).

Other activities which marked the first year of the new King James's were successful seasons in a wide variety of games – hockey, netball, cross-country, tennis, rounders, basketball, badminton, cricket, rugby, football and five-a-side soccer. There was a trip to Paris, a Walking Club weekend at Keld, and well-attended meetings by the Debating Society, Chess Club, Christian Union, Bridge Club and Stamp Club (run by Mr Gibbs). The Spoken English Competition was won by Andrew Watts, and drama gave us *A Doll's House* and *A Midsummer Night's Dream* as well as the Inter-house Drama Competition. Music also flourished, with orchestra, wind quartet, recorder consort, brass band and madrigal group. The high point was when Maurice Armsby, Head of Music, staged with an augmented choir a performance of Mendelssohn's *Elijah* – the first public concert to take advantage of the spacious Sports Hall, in March 1972. The following December there was a fine Christmas concert in S1, including

Newby House, the first overall winners of KJS Athletics Standards, 1972, with Newby House teachers, Mrs Nan Purvis, Mr Mike Jones and Mr Bob Gibbs.

the choir's hearty assurance: 'We all like figgy pudding!'. Also noteworthy in that year was the formation of the King James's Parent-Teacher Association, or the PTA, in May, 1972, with Mrs Belle Milnes as Hon Secretary.

The most notable event of the following year was the retirement, on the 13th April 1973, after 38 years of outstanding service, of Molly Sawdon. A tribute to her was paid in the school magazine by Nancy Beaumont, who quoted old pupils, such as Martin Minogue ('a rather stern and forbidding presence. . . but kind and soft-hearted. . . a great gift for fashioning astonishingly capable performances from the most pedestrian material') and Dr Kathleen Aberle (née Gough), the distinguished anthropologist, who spoke of how Miss Sawdon 'evoked a will to work, to think clearly and critically, and a wish to comprehend, not only grammar and literature, but the whole of life'. Mike Storr also wrote a handsome tribute, speaking of Molly's unfailing enthusiasm and thoroughness, her 'impatience with verbosity' and other invaluable qualities she had passed on to her pupils.

Miss Sawdon was replaced as Senior Mistress by Miss Margaret D Wilson, who had special responsibility for the Sixth Form and A Level exams, soon followed by the appointment of Mr K B Stone as Senior Master. He had special responsibility for the 'ROSLAS', those pupils, often resentful, who had to stay on an extra year because of the Raising of the School Leaving Age, and for whom Mr Stone introduced the City and Guilds exams in more practical subjects. Miss Wilson and Mr Stone were able to see the whole school, with the exception of the First Year, assembled in the Sports Hall for the very first Speech Day (Founder's Day) to be held there in October 1973. In those prefectorial days there was still a Head Boy and Head Girl performing the traditional task of reading extracts from the Letters Patent concerning the founding of the school in 1616.

In 1973 the school, now seeming more consolidated, continued with its various activities, noteworthy drama work being the Lower School's *Toad of Toad Hall* (produced by Mrs Wendy Harrison), the Middle School's *Peter Grimes* (produced by Mr Crosthwaite) and the Seniors' *The Crucible* (produced by Mr Storr) – as well as a joint production with the music department of the school opera *All the King's Men*. In November we organised the first of our satirical PTA shows, recordings of which still vibrate with uproarious laughter (Sample: playing the part of KJS boys we teachers parade before a pompous Matron for a 'nit inspection'. She announces: 'In this school one thing I will not tolerate is a dirty head!' Enter a bedaubed Mr Brewin, sportingly playing himself.)

Some groups and societies were now ranging far, helped by the provision by the PTA, under the chairmanship of Mr J Enticknap, of a school minibus. A second houseparty at Berwick-upon-Tweed was organised by the Christian Union, and a trip to Wales arranged by the Walking Club. One of the more interesting trips was the one to Germany in the Easter holidays, organised by Mr Hemsworth, Miss Fraser and the assistant, Dominique. This was to Mainz and Heidelberg, and a forerunner of the visits that would later be made to Knaresborough's twin town of Bebra.

The following year, in fact, in May 1974, there was the start of the long-lasting friendship between King James's and the Bebra school, the Brüder-Grimm Schule. The German party made the journey to Knaresborough, hosted by local families and spending some time with us during the school day. Organised by Alan Hemsworth, Head of German, this was the first of the many exchange visits, alternating between trips to Knaresborough and trips to Bebra, which have been a mainstay of town-twinning – thanks especially to the efficiency and enthusiasm of the English teacher, Herr Jochen Haase. In 1971 German had been taught only from the fourth year upwards, but now it was expanding to become an important second language to French, thanks partly to the Bebra link. This was well supported by language teachers such as Mrs Pauline Sibson, and most remarkably by Linda Baxter, who regularly led or accompanied visits to Bebra and hosted German teachers over more than 25 years. Like Mr Hemsworth, her contribution was recognised by the award of a gold medal by Bebra Town Council.

1974 also saw the publication of a *Handbook of Information for Staff* (February, revised September) edited by Mr Stone, Senior Master. This is of considerable historical interest in that it shows the kind of school that Mr Brewin had by this time established, and which he was preparing to hand over to the Head who would replace him when he retired the following year. In the section on the Lower School, for example, it is stated that entrants 'are placed in forms according to the alphabetical order of their surnames, I.1 to I.9.' The time-table included certain periods taken by these forms, but also others taken when they were divided into sets. This was rather complicated. Based on assessments received from the Primary Schools in English and maths, the first years started out in three kinds of sets, in order of apparent ability – 1 to 4, 5 to 8 and 9 and 10.

There were different common sets for French, history and geography, and also science. Forms through the school were arranged in pastoral groups, each with a teacher in charge, and Miss Crowther and Mr Simpson as senior Group Teachers. In addition there were Year Heads – Miss Hunter (Firsts), Mrs Winter (Seconds), Mr Crosthwaite (Thirds), Mr Herrington (Fourths) and Mr Mawdsley (Fifths). Third Year forms were arranged in order of academic ability, with IIIA1 and IIIA2 taking German or Latin, in addition to French. At the end of the Third Year examination subjects were chosen for O Level or up to six CSE subjects. Entry to the Sixth Form was open to everybody and did not depend on exam results.

The *Handbook* gives a detailed account of the responsibilities of Form Teachers, most important of which were the regular check on pupils during the registration period, the keeping of pink record cards and the writing of reports. Also noted was the fact that at lunchtime children were only allowed to stay inside the building if the green light and 'Inside' were displayed in inclement weather. If a red light was shown and they were allowed outside, they had to respond to the external bell rung at 1-35 pm. Morning assemblies were taken very seriously, with everybody required to attend, including staff, unless they had 'religious scruples which prevented their being present'. This did not apply to the four staff on duty, who patrolled the school during assemblies to round up stragglers and dodgers.

Also taken very seriously was staff detention, held every Tuesday from 3-50 to 4-50. The *Handbook* contains a full Code of Conduct and many other rules concerning uniform, school meals, school visits, the use of the library (under Mr 'Joss' Varley), fire regulations and so forth – all designed to produce a well-ordered community. The weakest point in any school day, of course, is if a class is left unsupervised. So it is always a matter of urgency to find a teacher to take the class of an absent colleague. The arranging of 'cover' or 'substitution' was usually carried out, often apologetically, by Mr Lancefield or Mr Stone, and it was always unpopular amongst the staff, especially if no work had been set.

There were various successful events in 1974, including another mock election we organised shortly before the country's General Election. Ours was in February, with four excellent candidates, who enlivened the school with their posters, banners, rosettes and heckling in the quads and corridors. As Alison MacIntyre commented in her magazine report: 'It was generally agreed that the most original campaign was that conducted by the Liberals, with their sandwich-boards and fancy hats. . . constantly engaged in battle'. The results anticipated the direction in which local politics was moving:

Michael Bland	(Conservative)	468
Louise Haylock	(Women's Lib)	47
Donald Page	(Liberal)	509
Tony Sleight	(Labour)	311

Other out-of-school activities continued to do well in 1974, especially in music and drama, including a popular comedy about suffragettes, *The Militants*. Music combined with drama to give us a wonderful performance of *Noye's Fludde*, given by the Lower School, with help from Aspin Park School, the whole replete with splendid masks and sets by the design department, and a convincing storm at sea. Noah was played by Mike Storr and a tipsy Mrs Noah unforgettably played by Madge Foster (RE and music). There was also much activity that year on the games field, which for the first time was the venue for the Claro Championships.

A fair number of students went on to university, polytechnics or colleges of education, though not as many as in the two previous years (23, as against 52 in 1973) and 47 passes at A Levels. The number who passed O Level (or the CSE equivalent) amounted to 64 (52 the previous year), most of these with six, seven or eight passes, and one with nine. Not an outstanding year, but the O Level/CSE results promised well for the future, and this year – which was to have been his final one before retirement – would have been quite a satisfying one for Mr Brewin.

However, at the Founder's Day in 1974, Councillor Holch spoke more than he knew when he said the day was tinged with sadness. Already we had said goodbye to Nancy Beaumont, an old girl of the school and one of our longest-serving teachers, praised by her younger colleague and fellow-pupil, Maggie Winter, for her stimulating teaching of English and unfailing cheerfulness. (Remembered affectionately, too, for her readiness with her fly-spray, which she carried around in summer, once being mystified by the number of wasps disrupting her lesson – all released in carefully-timed succession by certain boys from concealed match-boxes!) Now, after Mrs Beaumont, said Councillor Holch, the school must prepare to say goodbye to both Mr Walker and Mr Brewin.

The guest speaker, Sir Alec Clegg, ended his speech by congratulating Mr Brewin on 'his fine work as Headmaster of King James's.' It was good that he did. Within a couple of months the Headmaster had died – just a month before he would have taken his well-deserved retirement.

Noye's Fludde (1974), the first of two successful KJS productions. Left is Noah, played by Mr Storr, with Miss Madge Foster as Mrs Noah. The cast includes children from Aspin Primary School.

Early on that February morning, which happened to be Ash Wednesday, Mr Brewin was at his desk for his usual meeting with the senior staff, preparing to take the Sixth Form assembly he always referred to as 'prayers'. He suddenly collapsed with what later was found to be the bursting of an aneurysm in his brain – amounting to a massive stroke. His last words spoken in school, as they carried him out on a stretcher, were: 'But I must take prayers. . .'. He died in hospital the following day, the 13th February 1975.

A shock-wave ran through the whole school, a sense of horrible tragedy, and real compassion for Mrs Mary Brewin and their two sons. There was a tense and emotional atmosphere as Charlie Walker broke the news at the Middle School assembly. All over the school children were strangely silent, and some were in tears.

The funeral was held the following Monday, which was the start of the half term holiday. At a crowded and representative service in St John's Parish Church, where Mr and Mrs Brewin had been such loyal members, the Vicar, the Rev Ronnie McFadden, spoke movingly of Mr Brewin's Christian witness and his twenty years of single-minded, utterly dedicated work for the school, describing him as 'every inch a schoolmaster'. A further tribute appeared in the school magazine, referring to his 'high ideals and great integrity, his sense of mission, his moral and spiritual strength. . . No detail was too insignificant for his attention. Nobody in the school worked harder than its Headmaster.' In later years some who had been outspokenly critical of Mr Brewin, when they looked back, saw that he had indeed made a foundational contribution to King James's, perhaps even to the point of self-sacrifice, having exhausted himself through overwork.

This King James's Headmaster is unique in that he lies buried within the sight and sound of his old school in Knaresborough Cemetery. On his gravestone is inscribed a line from the Psalms so dear to Dr Chaloner: 'In Thy presence is fulness of joy'.

11. King James's: From Strength to Strength (1975-1997)

There was a strange, unreal atmosphere in the school when we returned for the second half of the spring term in 1975. Nothing seemed the same without the ever-present patriarchal figure of Mr Brewin, a conspicuous absence experienced especially by the senior teachers and office staff who had worked with him so closely. An essential element, largely taken for granted, was no longer here, and there were those in the school who felt curiously bereft. We had, of course, been preparing for a change following his forthcoming retirement, but not this untimely, dramatic departure.

Until the next Headmaster was ready to take over, the fort was held – for the rest of the term – by the Deputy Head, Mr Lancefield, who was already kept busy by his oversight of school meals, transport (buses to the villages), stationery and stock (now dispensed by Mr Nudds) and the organisation of O Level and CSE exams. Arthur, calling on his experience as Headmaster of Knaresborough Secondary Modern School, made a business-like job of directing King James's as acting head, in spite of the problems of an entire lack of ordered change-over that would normally have occurred. His style was that of a hands-on kind of manager – not sitting in isolation in his office, but often to be seen, and heard, about the school, keeping an eye on general discipline and standards. I once heard him shouting furiously at a boy who was misbehaving in the corridor outside the staff room:

'Absolutely disgraceful behaviour!', he roared. 'What's your name?' The offending boy mumbled his identity (and I don't think Arthur would mind my recalling the unconscious humour of the sequel) – and he then was told: 'Right! I'll *remember* that name! Shocking behaviour! Never seen anything like it!. . . *What* did you say your name was?'

The successor to Mr Brewin, starting in April 1975, was another Cambridge graduate, this time in history, Mr J E W Moreton. He had been the first Headmaster of Dinnington High School, South Yorkshire, one of the West Riding Education Committee's early 'flagship' comprehensives, with more than 2,000 pupils. When he arrived he was anxious that his conception of the term 'comprehensive education' should be fully understood by everybody, and to this end he immediately called a staff meeting, followed by an assembly of the entire school.

At the staff meeting he stressed that he considered all pupils to be of equal importance, and suggested that education should mean the intellectual, physical, spiritual/moral and aesthetic development of every pupil. This holistic approach would need to be as variable as the needs of each pupil and could only be achieved against a background of order and discipline and by the stimulus provided by a skilful and sympathetic staff. At the full assembly, Mr Moreton recalls that he spoke at considerable length of the standards he would expect to find in cleanliness, discipline, order in class and between lessons, good behaviour in the town, attendance, dress, courtesy and homework.

A few months after the new Headmaster's arrival one of the strongest links with the old Grammar School was severed by the retirement in July 1975 of Charles Walker, famed Head of Chemistry since 1938, and from 1971, Head of Middle School. We gave Charlie a triumphant send-off on the last day of the summer term, presenting him at morning assembly with a pair of binoculars. Somebody had said they were for bird-watching – but as I pointed out in the tribute, Charlie had been watching birds for years, and had managed very well without binoculars, especially when he selected strands from his favourite long-haired girls and grew crystals on them in the lab. No wonder King James's girls, regularly treated to Polo mints, used to sing, 'Charlie is mi darling'. At a dinner in the evening at the Red Lion, South Stainley, Charles and Mary were surrounded by colleagues and friends. One of the lines from a valedictory poem referred to the fact that 'now his white lab coat's for umpiring cricket', because he would henceforth have more time to serve his beloved Knaresborough Cricket Club, of which he was Captain of the First Eleven, and later President.

Mr Walker's key position as Head of Middle School was filled at the start of the summer term by Mr F D Winspear, who had taught under Mr Moreton at Dinnington. He was to become an important factor in continuity and stability, eventually serving King James's for 27 years.

The Middle School was, in fact, where the Mr Moreton felt reorganisation was essential, so that there was adequate support for the new Head of what was by far the biggest section of the school, with around 900 pupils, and where most of the ill-discipline and absenteeism was to be found, especially amongst those who were soon to leave school. Mr Moreton decided on a new pastoral structure by introducing a year system, placing each of Years 3, 4 and 5 under a Head of Year, with a Deputy of the opposite sex. They were to deal with day-to-day problems, referring anything serious to the Head of Middle School, who kept in close touch by holding regular meetings with the six Year Heads. Corporal punishment was still a final sanction, and was not, in fact, made illegal until the Education Act of 1986. Each form was given one tutorial period a week, when problems could be discussed and homework, uniform and general behaviour could be monitored. Homework was now based on a new homework diary, which proved very effective.

A similar system also applied to the Lower School, which since 1971 had been developed with commendable success through the hard work of Mr Andrews, the former Head of Boroughbridge Secondary School. Alas, Frank had struggled on in spite of the increasing health problems that finally brought about his death early in 1977. He was followed as Head of the Lower School by Mr David Jones, who came here from Germany, where he had considerable experience of teaching the children of servicemen in comprehensive schools. In the Lower School there were at first no Year Tutors, but Mr Jones had Mrs Winter as his Assistant Head for the girls, and Mr Phil Brown for the boys. Later there were Year Heads, such as Joan Silvester and Brian Fitzgibbon, with oversight of the First and Second Years.

Links were developed with contributing Junior Schools, Social Services, the School Attendance Officer, the Careers Service and so on. As a result of this, allied to the new pastoral structure, in the words of Mr Moreton, 'There were great gains in tone and dress, and in attendance and application to studies. . . The structure thus completed, the Headmaster delegated to the Heads of Lower and Middle Schools all the necessary authority.'

An important change amongst the seniors was that the old prefectorial system was abolished. Now all Sixth Formers were made prefects, the Headmaster being of the opinion that this reflected changes in society as a whole, where all young people of this age would soon have civil rights and responsibilities. There was now no longer any Head Boy or Head Girl, and the honours boards recording these, the games captains and the achievements of former pupils, were all removed during Mr Moreton's time. The prefects, as before, helped with supervision at break and lunch time, ran the school tuck shop, and had their own committee, overseen by Miss Wilson.

Spiritual and moral education was still seen as important at all levels, a lead being given by the Head of RE who had been appointed in 1974, the Rev H J Royston Emms, an experienced Methodist minister, who exerted a Christian influence both in the classroom and in assemblies. Three assemblies, each including prayers, were held every day (for the Lower and Middle Schools and the Sixth Form) often taken by the Headmaster. These ranged from the Lower School, where hymns were still sung, to the Sixth Form, where assemblies were frequently taken by Form Tutors, and where we now had freedom to experiment, producing some thought-provoking sessions.

Lower Sixth Netball teams (1975). Back from left: Elaine Renton, Janet Maude, Rachel Kellett, Catherine Ibbotson. Front: Liz Jackson, Andrea Lund, Angela Horsman.

UI6 Netball team (1998), Yorkshire and Humberside Regional Champions. Back, from left: Claire Farrow, Sally Dodgson, Penny Davison, Helen Carter. Front: Claire Marcroft, Charlotte Moore, Fiona Kemp.

The competitive spirit between the school houses continued as before, but the six were now reduced to four, with their names changed to those of Yorkshire dales:

Airedale   Nidderdale   Swaledale   Wharfedale

Essential to help with communication in such a large school were numerous meetings, such as the Monday morning gathering of the Headmaster, Deputy, Senior Master and Mistress and the Heads of Middle and Lower School (known to the office staff as 'MI 6'). This weekly meeting of senior staff reviewed all aspects of school life, establishing a horizontal link across the school to further the making and implementation of policy. In addition, there were full staff meetings for all the teachers, as well as departmental meetings. These were the days of long discussions and earnest debates, days characterised by a new awareness of educational theory and policy. Instead of the old-style 'lesson' we now had a 'teaching situation', and there was much talk of 'ethos', 'methodologies' and other items in the latest educationalese, my favourite being 'an injection in a specific area', referring to allocation of money.

Mr Moreton certainly made sure there was plenty of contact between the school and the wider world of educational thinking. His time here was notable for the number of courses he persuaded staff to attend, from those for heads of departments, at the University of York, for example, to special residential courses for the teaching staff, like those at Woolley Hall, Bramley Grange and Grantley Hall. In school there was still widespread use of 'chalk and talk' – though now mostly with roller-boards instead of the old fixed blackboards, and sometimes on whiteboards, with the new Nobo pens. But there was increasing use of aids such as tape-recorders, overhead projectors, films, radio and television, with Alec Dickson as full-time technician, as well as the various laboratory assistants. The school owes a lot to such workers, including in the early years Mr Frankland (who married one of our science teachers, Miss Sewell), and Mr Philip Fulcher. More recently we have had Mrs Janet Turner, Mrs Christine Parkin, who retired in 2002 after 25 years here, Christine Willoughby, a pupil in the 1970s, Greg Margerison and Alan Lever (Design and Technology) and Mr Derek Winter, site technician.

A change of nomenclature was made by Mr Moreton in the first three school years, with his introduction of three bands, each subdivided into four sets. Following discussions between the Head of Lower School and the headteachers of the contributing schools, pupils were placed according to their academic attainment at this stage into the bands, named Red, White and Blue, further, but equally, divided into groups named after the four points of the compass, so that we taught, for example, 1RS (1 Red South), 2BN (2 Blue North) and so on. This was considered to be a better system than the fine-setting of as many as ten different forms, which would have been too predictive at this stage. Moreover a watch was kept on pupils who could be moved into another band when it was considered desirable. PE, games and design were taken in mixed groups within the bands. The Third Years were more closely set, preparatory to choices being made for external exams.

Fully committed to the principles of comprehensive education, Mr Moreton believed that 'the acquisition of literacy and numeracy by the least able pupil was as important for that person as university admission for the most able.' He therefore not only valued the A Level high-flyers, but built up the department which had concentrated on children with learning difficulties and often the accompanying behaviour problems. As Mr Moreton and his family did not live in the Headmaster's house he persuaded the governors and the education authority to adapt this part of the school as a remedial centre for children with special needs. When Mrs Kirkham left (as Miss Oldman, she had married Mr Andrew Kirkham, Head of Physics), he appointed a new head of department, Mr Barry Wademan, whose team later included Mrs Jean Jones, wife of the Head of Lower School, and Mr Neville Green, who became Head of Special Needs when Barry Wademan left in 1980.

The most nerve-racking job in a school, especially in a large comprehensive, must surely be the making of the time-table. Mr Brewin, perhaps because of his mathematical interest, had always done this himself, never delegating any part of it. Now this infernally complex task was performed by Mr W H Jowsey, whose skill in chess, and so much else, made him, it was thought, an appropriate person to move around all those initialled sets, with the initials of the staff who would teach them. Covering the five days of the school week, his job was to allocate a great variety of teaching-groups to the 40 periods available, still taken as five in the morning (with break after the second) and three in the afternoon – changed in 1976 to four in the morning and four in the afternoon. This last change was to meet the demand for more double periods preferred in certain subjects.

Problems in the time-tabling were partly the result of a wider subject-choice being available. In the Middle School everybody took English, maths, a science and an aesthetic subject, with RE, PE and games. They were then allowed a choice of other subjects, with French for those with reasonable ability and German in addition, started in the Year Three for better linguists. This all led, of course, to pupils taking a programmme of exams at O Level, CSE, or a combination of both.

Mr Moreton laid particular stress on the development of aesthetic subjects, not only music, which was already well-established, but the combination of subjects in the Design Department led by Mr Kearney – art, woodwork, metalwork, needlecraft and home economics. He saw these as providing important opportunities to develop personal creativity and skill, as well as an appreciation of the artistic in all aspects of life. He was particularly gratified to find that

The Sixth Form with Mr Moreton and senior staff in 1981

Mr Gordon Allison, crafts inspector and later Senior Adviser for North Yorkshire, was full of praise for this aspect of the KJS curriculum and the fact that design was a compulsory subject up to Year Five. A pleasant outcome of this was that when Mr Allison was asked by the Chairman of the North Yorkshire County Council, Colonel Lawrence Jackson, if he could find pupils who would design and make a lectern for use at County Hall, he approached Mr Moreton, who through Peter Kearney and Mike Newsome, arranged for two boys in their exam year to undertake the project.

Various alterations were made in the way the Sixth Form was organised. Instead of the traditional division between arts and science forms (LVIA, LVIS etc) these were now mixed groups, for which Margaret Wilson organised a programme of General Studies, so that Sixth Formers spent a double period each Wednesday on activities such as drama and music. At this time also new Sixth Form tutor groups were made – all boys or all girls.

New subjects, such as European studies, were now being added experimentally to the curriculum. Economics, for the first time in the history of the school, was introduced into the Middle School and Sixth Form by Mr Moreton, who appointed for the purpose a second teacher from Dinnington, Keith Millett – soon known to us also as a keen rugby player. Economics proved to be a very popular subject, partly because of the way it was shown through newspapers and television to be a fundamental part of everyday life. Various trips were arranged, especially the annual visit to London, which included experience of the City and the Bank of England. Mr Millett also invited nationally-known politicians and economists to come to the school, including Merlyn Rees and Sir Keith Joseph, each of whom gave a talk and chatted with staff and pupils.

The most distinguished visitors of all – though they only drove slowly past the cheering, flag-waving school assembled along King James Road – were the Queen and the Duke of Edinburgh, on a Silver Jubilee visit to the area on the 12th July 1977.

Contact with the outside world was at its most practical in the various school trips to places of interest, many abroad. Now we had, in addition to the regular contact with Germany (Bebra) and trips to France, the first visit to Eastern Europe. This was to Prague in 1978, followed by one to Moscow in 1979, led by Don Winspear and Keith Millett. The school henceforth regularly organised trips to Russia, right up to the demolition of the Berlin Wall in 1989.

Close at hand were expeditions to a new outdoor education centre which Mr Moreton had been keen to establish in the hamlet of West Knapton (with important help from the George A Moore Foundation) on the A64, within easy reach of Scarborough and Filey. Here an unused school building, at a peppercorn rent of £1 a year, had been converted to become a residential base for courses and activities relating to the countryside and seaside, and was put to good use by Knaresborough's Junior Schools as well as King James's.

Cultural activities at school continued to flourish during the 1970s. For example, in December 1973 three plays were performed by the Sixth Form, including *The Visit* and *Spring and Port Wine* and in 1975 we presented an irreverent satire of school life in another hilarious PTA show. Music, always a strong tradition, prospered first under Mr Martin Hotton, then under Mr David Turmeau, with all kinds of performances, notably at the popular Carol Services, held in St John's Parish Church, filled to capacity by parents and the public. During those atmospheric evenings there were outstanding choral and instrumental items, including the school's home-made Hotton-Kellett carol, 'Good Old St Nicholas' (1975). The choirs and orchestra blended perfectly with traditional readings from the Festival of Nine Lessons and Carols – usually, and appropriately, in the King James's Authorised Version.

The school now had two orchestras, a military band, a brass group, string group, string quartet, junior choir, recorder group, swing band and a jazz group, the latter given an enthusiastic lead by Neville Green (piano) and Mike Wilkins (clarinet), the Acker Bilk of King James's. Musicians from the school also made an important contribution to the more ambitious performances of NYSSO (North Yorkshire Schools Symphony Orchestra) and HASSO (Harrogate and Skipton Schools Symphony Orchestra), in which Tim Kellett, later a member of 'Simply Red', was principal trumpet. One of David Turmeau's first productions, given three performances in 1977, was *Oliver*, in which the title role was played by Robin Van Zelst, Fagin by Robin Enticknap, and a chillingly brutal Bill Sikes by Mr Hemsworth. In drama we had *Twelfth Night* (1976), *The Caucasian Chalk Circle* (1977), *The Comedy of Errors* (1978) (exploiting the talents of the Davey twins), *Antigone* (1979) and *A Midsummer Night's Dream* (1981). Mr Storr also arranged a number of visits to performances of plays, mainly Shakespeare, in various towns, but especially Stratford.

Music once again joined with drama to provide a splendid production of *HMS Pinafore*, also in 1978, directed by Mike Storr. One of the invited guests was Sir Alec Clegg, who was heard to comment that this

Programme cover of *O what a Lovely War!* (April 1981), one of many designed by Mr Ron Burnett.

KJS Swing Band at the Scouts' Carol Concert (1978)
(Knaresborough Post)

was the best school production he had ever attended – high praise indeed coming from the venerable education chief. Benjamin Britten's cantata, *St Nicholas* (1978), was followed by another successful G and S, *Patience*, in 1979, with a full orchestra and a chorus of forty directed by Mr Phil Brown. Other great occasions were Offenbach's vivacious *Orpheus in the Underworld* (1980), also directed by Phil and, for something completely different, *O What a Lovely War!* (1981), directed by Colette Housego of the English department. Amongst Colette's other successes were the annual Sixth Form pantomimes, put on especially for Primary School audiences.

A full record of extra-curricular work during this period is difficult to compile because, following the death of Mr Brewin, there was no further publication of the *Chaloner* for another fifteen years. Some of the many school activities were, however, chronicled in an isolated publication, like a small school magazine, entitled *Melting Pot*, published in April 1979. This covered, amongst other things, trips, clubs, school productions and events such as the annual Christmas party, organised by the Sixth Form for Knaresborough's Senior Citizens. Four pages were devoted to work in PE, athletics and games, some of which had been disrupted by the collapse of the roof of the Sports Hall in January 1979. This had badly affected basketball, table tennis, badminton, trampolining, five-a-side soccer, weight-lifting and winter training for cricket and athletics.

Out of doors all went well, with the school being represented in the annual Claro-Craven Championships, the Yorkshire Championships, the England Championships, and winning the inter-school match at Granby High School. The soccer First Eleven reached the semi-final of the North Yorkshire County Competition and improvement was noted in the rugby First Fifteen, with two senior players, D Myers and P Sadler, representing North Yorkshire U16 Schoolboys. There were good results in basketball, gymnastics, swimming, cross country, hockey and cricket, the latter losing only its second game of the season when it provided a First Eleven, very narrowly defeated by a Staff Eleven.

Records of this kind, together with individual memories of a full and vibrant school life, in and out of the classroom, are evidence that during Mr Moreton's six years here the traditional King James's balance between academic and social activity was always of first importance. By now, few would dispute that this was a well-established Comprehensive School, one of the best in the area, with consistently good exam results. Mr Moreton had reached retirement age in 1980, but that year there were two important departures – those of Margaret Wilson (succeeded by Janet Newell), who left to become Headmistress of Maggie Thatcher's old school in Grantham, and Arthur Lancefield, who retired as Deputy Head after 30 years in teaching. So in order to help to maintain stability at senior level the Chairman of Governors,

Dr Stanley Hazel, persuaded Mr Moreton to stay on a further year. He accordingly retired at the end of the summer term, 1981, being presented with a fine oak table made by Mr Andy Wells of the woodwork department and a much-admired painting by Peter Kearney of Knaresborough Parish Church seen from over the Nidd.

Mr Moreton was invited to return the following April, when he unveiled a photograph of himself in the library, where it was placed adjacent to the one commemorating Mr Brewin – portraits of two very different personalities, each of whom had left his individual imprint on the school.

Different in style again was the next Headmaster, Mr J R Forster, whose appointment dated from September 1981. A graduate in English, and the fourth Cambridge man in a row to become Head, he came to us from the Salt Grammar School, Saltaire, Shipley, part of the community that is now a world heritage site, founded by Sir Titus Salt – who, incidentally, had once contemplated building his model mill-town on the banks of the Nidd at Knaresborough. Mr Forster, having previously been Deputy Head at Horsforth School, had been Headmaster at Salt's for six years. When he left, as caning was still part of the headmaster image, the local press referred to his time there with the headline 'Six of the best'.

Having settled in at Calcutt, Knaresborough, with his wife, Beryl, and their son and daughter, he first made a point of establishing good relations with the staff, including the office staff, led by Vera Cohen. He also wanted to try to remove the division he perceived between classroom teachers and pastoral officers. Though he was friendly and approachable, a Head with a human touch, it was not always going to be plain sailing as far as staff relations were concerned. There would eventually be prolonged conflict with the unions, as we shall see.

The new Headmaster brought with him certain clear principles that he wished to see observed throughout the school, summarised in a motto he introduced alongside the official one – 'Nothing but the best'. In particular he wanted to establish 'a civilised environment in which the nervous and gentle could flourish. . . and where the badges of aggressive and anti-social behaviour were not to be tolerated'.

In his own relationship with the children the Headmaster set out to be friendly, though firm. His tall figure and energetic style gave the impression that he was above all things a keen sportsman, essentially an outdoor type – but this, as he later pointed out, was a mistaken view, and no doubt originated from the fact that he was always willing to join in activities such as running. Though keen on sport, especially tennis, his interests were mainly in English language and literature.

The new Head's popularity with the children, of whom he had a total of 1,655, was not universal, and his tightening of regulations about uniform – banning boots and short trousers, for example – must have alienated a number of non-conformists. He had only been here a term when he received – more with amusement than alarm – a typed death-threat from the 'King James' Freedom Fighters'. They told him that he must hand in his resignation *'before Tues. 16 March or death will incurr. . .'* No doubt these were the same ungrammatical rebels who later daubed blood on the Head's study windows. Nevertheless the behaviour of King James's children, especially at lunchtime in the town, was soon seen to have greatly improved by Knaresborough Town Council, who sent the Head a letter thanking him for his disciplinary efforts. All those children, loosed on the town at lunchtime, tended to be an ongoing problem, and Mr Forster's introduction of policing by senior staff, especially with Don Winspear on his daily beat, later accompanied by Aidan Burbridge, was an important factor in monitoring behaviour.

Mr Forster's real problems struck him during the first term. A month or so after he arrived the expert on the all-important time-table, Howard Jowsey, was taken into hospital with a

The Headmaster, Mr J R Forster, as the school often saw him.

serious illness from which he never recovered. Howard, one of the most talented teachers in the history of the school, was fortunately replaced, in Latin, by his former pupil, now Mrs Janice Chatten, teaching part-time. His role as the school's time-tabler was taken over by Don Winspear, promoted by Mr Forster to the post of Deputy Head, alongside Janet Newell, the Deputy Head who had taken over from Margaret Wilson.

Though Don would eventually become 'site manager', dealing with the financial side of school life, as well as the nuts and bolts of the fabric, at this time these things were the Head's responsibility, and the source of many a headache. The School Log kept by Mr Forster records, along with all his dealings with people – governors, staff, pupils, parents, visitors, advisers, and so on – his dealings with material things essential to the smooth operation of the school. There was, for example, the flooding of the Design Block as a result of a leaking roof, followed early in his second term by the flooding of part of the school by a burst pipe. Then there were constant problems with the school boiler as it struggled – in spite of changes from coal to gas – to provide sufficient heating for the extensive campus.

The governors, as always, provided the Head with good backing, and were strengthened now by the election to their number of two staff-governors, Richard Watts and Peter Finan, and a parent-governor, Dr D A Beardsley. More fundamental changes in personnel, however, took place in Mr Forster's first few terms. There was the resignation of Matron, Mrs Hamilton (replaced by Mrs Barbara Crossley), and the departure of Keith Millett, who was appointed a Deputy Head at Granby High School, Harrogate. He was replaced by Mr Peter Leach as Head of Economics, later Head of Middle School, and by Mr Aidan Burbridge as Head of the Sixth Form, later with Mrs Audrey Houlston as his assistant, followed by Mrs Joyce Woods and Mrs Eileen Minshall.

One of the biggest problems concerning staff – though it meant an excess of teachers rather than shortages – was the opening of Boroughbridge High School, at first an 11-16 comprehensive, in the very September of 1981 that Mr Forster had taken over. Falling rolls at King James's were an immediate issue, with the loss, between 1981 and 1986, of about 400 pupils and 22 members of staff. However, this meant that opportunities opened up for early retirement and for promotions of younger staff, as well as for a general improvement in working conditions for both staff and pupils. Mention should also be made of Mr Forster's introduction of the Local Management of Schools scheme, which meant the freedom to control the school's own budget and establish financial security under Don Winspear.

In addition to sorting out its own affairs King James's found time to become involved with projects in the wider world. One of these was a revival of the school's traditional interest in Guide Dogs for the Blind, when the Lower School, on 19th February 1982, presented the association's regional manager with a cheque for £550, so they could sponsor and adopt a labrador called Mindy, henceforth to be known as 'the King James's Guide Dog.' Visits by pupils from Henshaw's School for the Blind, incidentally, as well as by handicapped pupils from the Ian Tetley School, were included in the General Studies course as part of social outreach.

In June 1982 we welcomed into the school, for a stay of ten days, our very first group of French exchange pupils – 26 with their teachers – from a school in La Roche sur Yon, Vendée. The following spring we took a group there on a successful return visit, led by Lynn Buller, Paul Conway, my wife and myself. From this time also there was a popular day-trip to Boulogne organised by Don Winspear, Linda Baxter and others. There were other school trips abroad, including our regular Bebra exchange. But the most interesting venture of all was the establishing of an off-shoot of King James's School in Africa.

This was in the little village of Mongegba in Sierra Leone, fifteen miles inland from Freetown, which our Deputy

Our African outpost - King James's School, Mongegba, Sierra Leone. A primary school off-shoot founded in 1983, and supported by KJS Knaresborough ever since.

Head, Ken Stone, happened to visit when he had permission to go on a tour of school inspection for the Methodist Church. He found this little community of poor woodcutters and charcoal burners in desperate need of a school, and on his return to Knaresborough set about raising £50, which he sent to Mongegba – sufficient for them to build a little school themselves, to accommodate thirty pupils. This was followed by King James's agreeing to raise about £350 a year to pay the salaries of two teachers at Mongegba, and King James's School, Knaresborough has ever since 1983 maintained contact with the grateful name-sake primary school in Sierra Leone.

A few years later, in 1988, the first visit to the Mongegba school was made by two Sixth Formers, Simon Thompson and James Stubley, where they did voluntary work as teachers. They reported difficult conditions because of politcal and economic instability, and described the abject poverty amidst the glorious scenery and lush vegetation, with its abundance of fruit. When a welcome consignment of books and paper arrived, sent by the Knaresborough King James's School, it was noticed that even the wooden crates were put to use as desks. The gratitude of teachers and children for support from England was reflected in one of the school songs in which the 'Mighty King James's Leader' was given the kind of praise normally reserved for saints in heaven:

> I will see King James's School in Knaresborough
> When I go to the Glory Land;
> I will see Mr Forster in Knaresborough
> When I go to the Glory Land!

In September 1992 another Sixth Former, Garry Jackson, went out to Mongegba, supported by £4,200 raised by the school and all kinds of well-wishers, including the novelist Catherine Cookson. He taught English and maths for a few months, helped to repair the inadequate mud hut of a school, and then set about securing land on which a new one could be built. Eventually, Plan International agreed to build a school for sixty children on a five-acre site, consisting of three classrooms, an office and a store. Appropriately present at the official opening in November 1997 was Ken Stone, along with the local MP, the headman of Mongegba and the Rev Amudu Sesay, the Headteacher since the school started. The position today is that King James's School, Mongegba, with its own green uniform, which proudly bears the King James's School badge, has grown to a total of 236 pupils and five teachers, their salary still paid by KJS Knaresborough.

A continued improvement in relationships with Knaresborough itself was one of Mr Forster's objectives in the 1980s. King James's was to be seen as part of the local community, and not an isolated educational enclave which happened to be located in the town. The most successful move in this direction came in 1983 when the famous Fun Run was started. The idea arose when a friend suggested the idea to Dr Beardsley, then Chairman of the PTA. It was enthusiastically supported by the Headmaster, an active participant from the beginning. Designed to raise money for King James's and for charity (in 1991, for example half the £5,000 raised went to the Mongegba project), the Fun Run was first held on Sunday, the 24th April 1983, with 520 sponsored runners covering courses of 2.5, 5 or 10 miles. Within a few years the entries had doubled, and the Fun Run was established as an annual event for the whole community and marked by a happy atmosphere, linked with a different theme each year which influenced the costumes. In 1990, for example, the theme was 'Simply Red', with our ex-pupil member of the group, Tim, as the opener and Mr Forster dressed as a giant red tomato. The following year the theme was 'Green', with the Headmaster running, this time dressed as a Ninja Turtle. Mr Forster was a genuine runner, and had taken part in the London Marathon, but his willingness to discard his dignity and give a lead by entering into the full spirit of the Fun Run will long be remembered.

As well as running for fun, standard games and athletics continued to be taken seriously under the steady leadership of Mr Bob Hearld, for the boys, assisted by Mr Jim Weatherill, and, over the years, many others busy in the gym and on the games field. As Head of Girls PE, we had Jean Ricketts (later Mrs Jean Brake), and then Mrs Pauline Bolton (1976-1996), assisted by teachers including Jan Coates and staff wives Mrs Sue Finan and Mrs Viv Mroviec. By the 1990s King James's was regarded as a leading school in the county for football, netball and tennis. The First Eleven did well in the West Yorkshire Merit Table under Mel Mrowiec, then Gordon Ibbotson, and the girls' netball teams twice represented Yorkshire in the national finals. In athletics Robin Simpson and Martin Chatten represented Yorkshire, Martin later becoming President of Durham University Athletics Association.

Arising from the Headmaster's special interest in tennis, a new Knaresborough Tennis Club was founded in 1985, with junior clubs at the school. Later, during the 1990s, school senior tennis teams reached national finals on four occasions, twice with boys, twice with girls, King James's being the only state school represented on each occasion.

In May 1982, as part of the policy of developing the integration of the school with the surrounding community, a special evening was arranged for the leaders of local industry, 27 of whom were guests of the staff. It is worth listing the teachers who met them and outlined the work-orientated nature of their departments: Mrs M B Barnes (computer studies), Mr A M Burbridge (economics), Mrs J Clarke (home economics), Mr N Clarke (design), Miss J Dawson (maths), Mrs W M Harrison (English), Mr K Hall (economics), Mr T M Jones (City and Guilds, engineering and physics), Mr J List (chemistry), Mr J Mawdsley (Head of Careers), Mr M Newsome (Head of CDT), Mrs A Thomas (maths), Mr P Walters (engineering and physics), Mrs S Ward (Head of Home Economics), Mr M J Wilkins (Head of Maths), Mr J Wilson (Head of Science). Contact with industry worked in the other direction, too, with a visit, for example, of thirty Sixth Formers the following year to the chemistry section of the CEGB laboratories, Harrogate. Other aspects of the links of the wider community were the

Staff of King James's School in July 1982, at the end of Mr Forster's first year as Headmaster.

bringing together of the youth service, adult education and leisure services in the Community Education Programme. The Further Education Centre, since 1971, had been part of the school campus, and now its facilities were opened up to people of all ages, later under Roger Linfoot, District Community Tutor.

As always, there was an opportunity for the general public to see what the school could do when it opened its doors for productions in drama and music, led by Mr Storr and Mr Turmeau respectively. Especially enjoyable were the polished performances of *Iolanthe* (March 1982), conducted by David Turmeau, and directed by Phil Brown. On the last night a presentation was made to Mr Brown, soon to retire after his many Gilbert and Sullivan productions. There was the double bill of *The Fire Raisers* and *Amahl and the Night Visitors* (December 1982), *Nets* (written by pupils and directed by Mr Mike Haining) and a further performance of *The Militants* (1983), with another PTA show at the end of the year. A classic play, T*he Importance of being Ernest*, directed by Mike Storr, and a pop musical, *Smike*, directed by Henry Ayrton, conducted by Kevin Box, were produced in 1984. *Dazzle* followed in 1985 and *When we are Married* in 1986. The appointment of Lisa Garside to teach drama led to adventurous productions such as *Absurd Person Singular* and *The Mikado*, both in 1987. Then came *The Visit* (1988) and the school's excellent second version of *Noye's Fludde*, along with *All the King's Men* and *See How they Run* (a staff play) all in 1989.

There is no space here to list all the actors and performers in these stage productions, and recourse will have to be made to surviving programmes and accounts in later editions of the *Chaloner.* It should, however, be noted – because voluntary after-school work can easily be taken for granted – that programmes and publicity were usually produced by Ron Burnett, scenery by Peter Kearney, with the lighting and amplification efficiently handled over many years by Mike Wilkins. A similar creative effort went into the life-size exhibits of the 'History through the ages' display organised by Mr Kearney in 1983.

Musical performances in the 1980s, too many to mention in detail, were of the usual high standard. Dave Turmeau, assisted by Pauline Cuss, Pat Livingstone and Kevin Box, presented regular concerts each spring, summer and autumn, including a variety of soloists on strings, woodwind and brass. The music department also provided programmes for the Lower and

Middle School prizegivings and Founder's Day, with the school Carol Service as the grand finale. In addition, there were special choral items, such as the joint performance, with The Mount School, York, of Fauré's *Requiem* in York Minster and the television appearance of the early-music group 'King James's Musicke Band'.

The evening of Founder's Day was by now the occasion for all kinds of activities put on to show the school in action to parents and other visitors. In October 1981 and 1982, for example, they could wander round and see sample lessons in progress in every department, with displays of course-books and equipment. There were scientific demonstrations and experiments in chemistry, physics, biology and engineering science. There was a demonstration of secretarial work and in the Design Block woodwork and pottery, drawing, painting and printing in progress, with the Home Economics department demonstrating needlework and the making of cakes.

The PE department organised indoor games and displays. The modern languages department held demonstration lessons in French and German and organised a really atmospheric French Café in the Further Education lounge. The menus were in French, and we insisted that all our waiters and waitresses responded only to orders in that language before they delivered food and drink, which was as authentically French as we could make it.

Though Mr Forster, in his early years, made few changes to the traditions and structures of the school, he had to contend with an unusual number of staff changes, mainly the departure of the 'old guard' who had the opportunity of taking early retirement. At the end of the summer term in 1982 the school said goodbye to Phil Brown, Terry Sayles, who had taught at King James's for 30 years, and Howard Jowsey, now seriously ill, who had taught here for 33 years. The following summer another three old-timers took early retirement – Vera Hunter, Raymond Nudds (33 years) and myself (27 years). The date was the 14th July, and I remember celebrating my own new-found freedom by singing '*La Marseillaise*' at our evening farewell party. A few days earlier we had held a final *Chez Arnaud* café with parasol tables in the quad, French accordion music, dancing to the Jazz Band and performances of a ravishing can-can performed by choice young lady teaching-colleagues.

A year later yet more staff took early retirement. At break on the last day of term in 1984 there were presentations to five teachers who had been at the school for just a few years, but in the evening there was a farewell gathering for long-serving ladies Betty Crowther, Margaret Grint, Marjorie Sayles and Sheila Ward, and three long-serving men, Ken Gregson, Richard Watts and John Wilson. In December of the same year – when, incidentally, it was announced that the school had seven Oxbridge acceptances – there was the retirement of Frank Griffin from the maths department and Janet Newell, Deputy Head, who left to become Headmistress of the Ripon secondary school that later became Ripon College. The following summer saw the departure of another Deputy Head, Ken Stone, Ann Mettam

Long-serving staff leaving King James's (July 1984). From left: John Wilson, Mrs Marjorie Sayles, Ken Gregson, Richard Watts, Mrs Margaret Grint. Front: Betty Crowther, Mrs Marjorie Hudson, Mrs Sheila Ward. *(Knaresborough Post)*

and Wendy Harrison. It was not just that these teachers had long and honourable service, but all were heads of departments or held senior positions.

There were changes too, in the office staff. In April 1982 Mrs Di Hurst, the bursar, a popular and familiar figure, entered hospital for an operation, and later had to retire. She was replaced by Mrs Janet Firth as bursar. Mrs Pat Beardsley, appointed to a temporary secretarial post in 1983, became, along with Mrs Margaret Darley, an almost permanent fixture in the office. Mrs Beardsley was appointed Secretary to the Head in 1988. Another long-serving worker in the office and library, Mrs Marjorie Hudson, retired in 1984, adding to departures ranging from that of the audio-visual technician, Tim Plaice, to the retirement of Miss Brenda Baines after 31 years as a governor.

The making of new appointments, together with internal adjustments and promotions, is obviously an important part of a Headmaster's work. Mr Forster, like his predecessors, seems to have made wise choices in maintaining a well-qualified and competent staff. Unlike previous Heads, however, he encountered problems with the national teachers' unions, through the industrial action which was affecting schools throughout the country. Though Mr Forster had strong sympathies with the demand for better pay, he felt it his duty to protect and supervise the children whose classes had been cancelled, rather than send them off the school premises – even though this was seen by staff as negating their strike action.

The first of these industrial actions came in March 1982, in his second term here, when the unions exercised 'a withdrawal of goodwill'. In the spring term of 1984 there was an NAS strike involving 32 teachers at King James's, which meant that 625 pupils had to be sent home early. The following term Years Three and Four were kept at home because of strike action, this time by members of the NUT.

Shortly afterwards came a lightning strike by the NAS, when six teachers were withdrawn at short notice each half day for a week. Early in 1985 NUT members again took action in connection with pay claims, and the NAS held a half-day strike which affected nearly 700 children. Then, in the summer term, industrial action was taken not only by the NUT and NAS but by the less militant AMMA members, who withdrew from taking lunch-time duties. There were half-day strikes, 'rolling strikes', 'days of action' and the withdrawal of all voluntary out-of-school activities. The disruption to school life became quite serious when there was joint strike action by the NUT and NAS, and the Head felt it necessary to close the school for half a day.

Feelings ran particularly high when the NUT representative accused the Head of using dinner-ladies to break the strike. There was a critical letter in the press and an anonymous letter from a member of staff. By an odd coincidence there was, throughout the strike action, the additional frustration of constant trouble with the temperamental school boiler, which – true to form – was generating far less heat than the strike.

The resumption of the boiler saga was a kind of sinister prelude to the collapse and sudden death of the Caretaker, on the 31st January 1986. Bill Sleight had done the demanding job of looking after the school for 17½ years, along with his wife, Dot, who had done so much on the catering side. He was honoured at an evening memorial service in the School Hall, when we remembered how Bill had kept the school in order for so long and beautified it with flowers. His memorial was the school building itself.

King James's gradually recovered from this rough passage. Relationships improved and new appointments were made – from Brian English, promoted to Caretaker, to John Midgley, appointed Deputy Head. The previous summer Mr Forster had shown that, in spite of the unsettling nature of the strike, the school had weathered the storm sufficiently to maintain its academic standards. In a letter to the *Knaresborough Post* he pointed out that 58 candidates had achieved 175 passes, giving a very creditable pass rate of 82%, with 35% of these in the top two grades. Five Sixth Formers had places at Oxbridge, and the O Level results were the best for some years, with 836 passes, achieved by a smaller Fifth Year, 45 of whom had eight or more passes. The 1986 results were also very good – 81.3% A Level passes and 627 at O Level.

The school continued to place great emphasis on careers and had strong links with local industry and employment. As part of this approach King James's had for four years run its own Farm Project, based on the rural science department, headed by Mr Ian Simpson. On the school premises the children could have first-hand experience of feeding and rearing hens, geese, turkeys, lambs, calves, goats and pigs – the whole project run like a business, and well supported by the Knaresborough Young Farmers, Rotary, Hutton's, the local butchers, and a £2,000 donation from the George A Moore Foundation, followed by a further donation of £5,500 in 1988, with Mr Moore himself opening the Animal House in June 1989. When Ian Simpson left in 1989 to become a lecturer at Bishop Burton College of Agriculture the management of the farm was taken over by Mrs Beryl Forster, the Headmaster's wife, who for many years had this role along with the farm technician, Jan Wilson.

Of the extra-curricular activities, all of educational value, we might mention another mock election, this time in 1987, which had the interesting result:

James Todd (Alliance Party)	287
Lee Fudge (Conservative)	249
Simon Thompson (Labour)	87

This can be compared with a later mock election, in 1994, in which Robert Harrington gained a victory for the Conservatives. Robert went on to become President of that most famous of debating societies, the Oxford Union, in 1997. This was the year of another school election inspired by Newsround, which produced results of Conservatives 41%, Labour 38% and Liberal Democrats 21%.

An important break with the earlier King James's School came on the 31st August 1988 when Vera Cohen retired after 28 years as Headmaster's Secretary – somebody always there, always unflappable, a fount of knowledge. At her well-attended retirement party we talked of how greatly such a pillar of the establishment would be missed – and of what secrets this genial but discreet lady would take with her into retirement.

Three sisters from the seventies at the Old Pupils' Reunion, October 1988

The summer of 1989 saw more changes in the teaching-staff, with the early retirement of Don Briggs, Head of Biology since 1960, and Peter Kearney, Head of Art and Design since 1970. Both Mr Briggs and Mr Kearney had not only been faithful and industrious teachers, but had played a full part in school life, giving valuable support to many stage productions, for example. David Baccus took over as Head of Art until he left a year or so later, then Mrs Biddy Noakes was appointed. She happened to be the daughter of the famous veteran actor, Sir Bernard Miles, and this led to an interesting coincidence. A pupil called Tom Palmer told the Head that a Christmas number of *Radio Times* had a cover picture of two characters from *Treasure Island* – Long John Silver, played by the father of his art teacher, and Jim Hawkins played by this boy's own father.

From 1990 the task of writing a chronicle on the school becomes so much easier with Mr Forster's revival of the *Chaloner*. This arose phoenix-like from the ashes of the old magazine, which had last appeared in 1975. And what a contrast it made with the earlier version! For one of the old pupils' reunions I organised, in October 1988, I had managed to assemble a complete set of *Chaloners* from 1932 onwards. How those present enjoyed thumbing through the nostalgic pages, comparatively dull though they were, with few illustrations! This brand-new *Chaloner* was very different in style, an A4 size glossy magazine, full of photographs, and well designed and presented.

This 1990 *Chaloner* devotes many of its pages to looking back over the years, including an account of a Founder's Day drama touching on the history of the school. This had first been tried in 1982, when the Second Year had reminded us of the school's history in a kind of choral reading, extended across the Sports Hall. In October, 1983, I celebrated my retirement by writing a humorous dramatisation for Founder's Day, involving Guy Fawkes as well as James I and Dr Chaloner. This was presented in 1983 and 1984, with a new version in 1985. Then it became a Founder's Day tradition, evolving out of all recognition, with lots of original and contemporary features, but still preserving a reminder of the past.

In other ways this first revived *Chaloner* gives a picture of school life at the beginning of the last decade of the twentieth century. There are accounts of trips abroad – to the Soviet Union, Austria and Normandy – of the performances in drama and music, and the achievements in girls' games, cross country, football, rugby, tennis and in house competitions, which included swimming, and came to a climax on Sports Day, which in 1989 had been won by Nidderdale. The summer of 1990, incidentally, saw the retirement of Jim Weatherill, a KJGS boy from 1946 to 1953, who had replaced Bob Hearld as Head of PE (he was now teaching full-time maths) and had served as a teacher at Knaresborough Secondary Modern School and King James's for a total of 31 years. He was succeeded by Mr David Lloyd and later by Mr Eddie Churchill. Also in 1990 there was a loss to the school in the departure of Mrs Audrey Houlston (English) who had joined the staff as Miss Jefferson in 1977.

In 1990 the school was glad to see, just at the other side of the road, the opening – after long campaigning – of Knaresborough Swimming Pool. This, though excellent in itself, has not turned out to benefit King James's in the way that was expected. For the first two years it was used for swimming lessons, but these were discontinued because of costing and lack of flexibility. The National Curriculum, incidentally, prescribed swimming only up to the last year of Primary schools. The annual Swimming Gala organised by King James's still took place, but instead of being across the road it was held at the pool in Harrogate Ladies College. Sport in general was doing well. Mark Dodd, for example, was chosen to represent England at U 16 Rugby in 1993, Melissa Reynard represented her country in Women's Cricket, as did Vicky Simpson, an Olympic skier – and Darren Manning's early go-karting led to his career as an ace racing-driver. The addition to the staff of Mr Steve Merifield, a player with the Premier League, meant a great boost for school basketball.

Though KJS was in a generally flourishing condition as it entered the 1990s, there were still areas needing attention. A level results in 1988 had reached their lowest point for some years, though in the same year the first-ever results in the new GCSE exam, replacing O Level, were exceptionally good, with 811 passes, grades A to C, and 92 candidates with five or more passes. Teaching was strengthened by the appointment of various new staff, including Paul Keogh (French) and Rob Snow (history). On the other hand there was the departure in 1991 of Stuart Herrington, Head of Chemistry, and like his mentor, Charlie Walker, a keen cricketer. Stuart, an old boy of King James's Grammar School, had first come to teach here in 1965, and had been head of department for the last 19 years. At the same time David Turmeau, Head of Music, left to take a similar post at the Queen Elizabeth School in Wakefield. His 14 years at King James's will be remembered for the enthusiastic lead he gave to so many musicians and singers, encouraged by his humour and panache.

A departure of a very different kind was the sudden, tragic death of Pearl Taylor in March 1991. Pearl had taught French here for almost four years and was a charming and dedicated young teacher, fully involved in school trips, careers education, netball and so much more. Her popularity and the immense sense of loss suffered by the school was expressed at a special thanksgiving service held in Holy Trinity Church. One of the creative pieces of writing which regularly appeared in *Chaloner* was a moving little poem entitled 'Miss Taylor' written by Catriona MacRae of Year 4.

Life goes on – and, on a lighter note, in the French department there was a trip to Paris, another to Normandy, as well as the Yorkshire-Lille exchange, and there was soon to be the first of a series of visits by staff footballers to the town of Bourges, the team being happily named *Allez, les profs!* In 1990 and 1991 old pupils achieved especially good results, with Firsts at Cambridge for Nick Fretwell, Jeremy Hornby and Martin Clayton, the latter moving on to a prestigious post as Deputy Curator of Prints and Drawings at the Royal Library, Windsor.

Closer to home, West Knapton was still in use, and the base for a very successful field trip led by Head of Geography, Mike Jones. Another Mr Jones, Malcolm, was in charge of work experience, responsible for getting pupils into work placement, so they had practical contact with local firms. By the end of the Fourth Year 200 pupils were going out for two weeks in some kind of employment. Related to this was the production from the beginning of 1991 of a Record of Achievement for each leaver, which was seen as something far more useful than the traditional school report. The third Jones on the staff retired in 1992, David Jones, who had been Head of Lower School for 15 years, with his wife, Jean, who had taught here, mainly Special Needs – and also run the fund-raising tuck shop – for 14 years.

School in the nineties maintained its cultural activities. The art department, for example, led by Mrs Biddy Noakes, organised an art exhibition which was supported by British Gas, who gave generous financial support. Four pupils spent a week at Castle Primary School painting a mural. The music department's notable successes were first, the home-spun musical *Dreamtales,* based on Arthurian legends, with text by Lisa Garside and music by Judith Kimber, then in 1992, after Bryan Western was appointed Head of Music, performances by the King James's Riverside Jazz Group, the Dixieland Band, the Chamber Choir, and an impressive range of individual successes in the Associated Board exams for clarinet, drums, flute, guitar, oboe, organ, piano (21 passes, 4 with distinction) recorder, saxophone, singing, strings (20 passes) theory, trombone and trumpet.

In drama Mr Storr, coming to the end of his own long run, directed a highly-acclaimed performance of *The Crucible* in 1992 – almost twenty years after directing the same play (notable for its ear-splitting shrieks) as one of his first productions in the Comprehensive School. The following year he watched Lisa Garside's direction of the challenging *Waiting for Godot.* Mike Storr retired in December 1992 after 27 years of teaching English and drama here, making a memorable contribution to the culture and continuity of the school. The high standard of direction he had maintained ever since the days of Molly Sawdon was continued by others – Annie Rose, for example, with her enthusiastically-received version of *A Midsummer Night's Dream* in February 1994.

In September 1993 Mike Wilkins, Head of Maths, retired. He had been here for 23 years, not only a lively teacher, but one who generously gave his time and talents to support jazz and swing, playing clarinet or piano. He also spent countless hours literally behind the scenes, working his electrical and electronic wizardry. At the same time Peter Whitehead, for health reasons, relinquished his role as Deputy Head, work he had done with distinction for nearly eight years, to return to the classroom as a part-time maths teacher. Margaret Slights also retired at this time. Having been Secretary to Arthur Lancefield she had been part of the office team, but had more recently been happily employed in the school library.

Looking back to 1974, scrolls are signed (November 1994) to commemorate the 20th anniversary of exchanges between KJS and the Brüder-Grimm Schule, Bebra. From left: Jochen Haase, Ulrike Kaschel, Linda Baxter, Alan Hemsworth.

Staff come and go, but the children in general seem to continue much as before, looking more or less the same as before, for the most part healthy and well-fed. A factor in this was school dinners. Ever since the days of Maud Scurrah the school has enjoyed good catering, thanks to long-serving Cooks-in-charge, like Mrs Pat Godbold, appointed in 1977, and dinner-ladies such as Mrs Betty Steele, who started way back in 1969.

To the majority of teachers the children were still 'pupils', but they were being referred to more and more as 'students', and the long-established system of grading them according to their years in secondary school was now officially altered – to the confusion of some, who had to keep extracting six from the number that was used. This new way of numbering, going back to the Education Act of 1988, was based on the idea that there was no discontinuity between primary and secondary education, so children now started at King James's, not in the First Year, but Year Seven. First used in the *Chaloner* of 1993, the labelling showed that the following evolution had taken place:

First Years → Year One → Year Seven → (and so on)

The Lower Sixth became Year Twelve, the Upper Sixth, Year Thirteen – and yet the old term 'Sixth Form' fortunately, though illogically, survived.

Within the school years the setting had also changed, parallel to the National Curriculum, introduced in 1988, followed by the new Key Stages. In 1989 the last of the old Red, White and Blue banding system was dismantled, and a common curriculum was introduced. There were now tutor groups in each year, based on the school houses, and continuing provision for those with special needs. There was a general expectation that any pupil with reasonable ability and motivation would go on to become a student in the Sixth Form, where eventually it was possible to choose from around twenty subjects at A or AS Level, or take GNVQ exams, or improve grades in GCSE exams. In September 1996 the Comprehensive School at Boroughbridge started its own Sixth Form, but numbers at KJS were not significantly reduced.

Three tragic deaths by accident hit the school around this time. Christopher Unwin, aged 16, in December 1994, Mr Ernie Marvin, popular Caretaker since 1992, in January 1995, and Michael Duddles, aged 13, in March 1995. Not long afterwards, the school acutely

Macbeth (1996) with Mark Leith in the title-role, and the three witches (from left clockwise) Rachel Shirley, Amy Walls and Emma Moger. *(Knaresborough Post)*

felt the loss of a former pupil, Michele Clayton, who from her wheelchair had opened the 1996 Fun Run.

The fact that King James's School had reached heights of excellence in the 1990s was unequivocally shown, first, by the presentation of the Investors in People Award in 1995. This, which entitled the school to use the special logo, was a highly-valued status symbol, given only to those firms and establishments with a sufficiently high standard in training and management, for the staff in general, not just teachers. King James's had the distinction of being the first secondary school in North Yorkshire to receive the accolade of Investors in People.

The second mark of distinction was the Ofsted Report of October 1996. This was produced after 13 government inspectors had descended on the school, probing into every corner of its life, sitting in on 300 lessons, attending all assemblies, examining the written work, holding discussions with staff, parents and the Chair of Governors. The result of their inspection was summarised in such glowing passages as the following:

> Very high standards are attained, enhanced by excellent facilities. Achievements of all kinds are recognised and celebrated. Pupils are valued as individuals. Their conduct, commitment and enthusiasm, initially very good, progressively improve throughout their years in school. The curriculum provides very well for all pupils of different abilities. The range and quality of extra-curricular provision is outstanding. Throughout the school the standard of teaching is quite exceptional.

It was noted that the number of staff at the time was 98, equivalent to 92.4 full-time teachers, with a pupil-teacher ratio of 16.29 to 1, roughly the national average. High praise went not only to the teachers, senior management team and the governing body, but to Mr Forster himself, of whom the Ofsted report said: 'For the last fourteen years the school has enjoyed the leadership of a Headteacher of great vision, energy, courage and dedication.' The inspectors especially appreciated the school's sense of tradition. 'It is evident in the distinctive effect of the different tartan worn by pupils at each Key Stage and by students in the Sixth

Form. This enhances the sense of identity of the school and fosters the pride and care taken by pupils and students in smart and often stylish appearance'.

The picture in the Ofsted Report of a school with so many good things to offer is borne out by the *Chaloners* of the closing years of the Forster regime, in 1996 and 1997. Here we can read of a wealth of activity, most of it quite unrelated to the eternal preoccupation with exam results . . . visits to London, Paris, Amsterdam, Boulogne and, of course, Bebra, with ski trips to Austria and canoeing in the Ardèche . . . instrumental music and singing . . . a performance of *Macbeth* . . . a visit by Norman Lamont, and a political opinion poll . . . Book Week. . . the Fun Run (1996) to raise money both for the school Information Technology and St. Michael's Hospice . . . tennis, squash, volley-ball, netball, athletics, gymnastics, aerobics, cricket, soccer and rugby – and now angling, which entered two teams, with Rob Ingledew being awarded the Angler of the Year prize . . . visits to mosques, biology field trips to Malham Cove and Wilstrop Farm . . . the Duke of Edinburgh Award . . . news of old pupils . . . and farewells to staff who had served the school long and faithfully – the Rev Roy Emms, John Midgley, Chris Edwards, Joan Silvester, Win Allison and Biddy Noakes, replaced by Mr Simon Crawford.

The most significant leaver was the Headmaster himself, who retired (to his home in Knaresborough) at the end of the Easter term, 1997, his main leaving-present being a fine bookcase, inscribed with his motto 'Nothing but the best', made by a former pupil, David Clegg, who had been trained as a craftsman by Mr Andy Wells and the Mouseman firm at Kilburn. In the *Chaloner* of that year there was a predictable reference to Mr Forster's long-distance running and his once having got lost in the London Marathon . . . Then the comment: 'Still, one race he managed to complete was the marathon of running King James's, and I am sure we would all agree that he finished in style'.

12. King James's: Gateway to the Future (1997-2003)

As Mr Forster had retired at the end of the Easter term 1997, Don Winspear served as acting Headmaster for the summer term. He was supported by Dr Carole Walton, who moved up to act as Deputy, later becoming Second Deputy Head, while Mr Winspear continued as the First Deputy Head.

In September 1997 King James's embarked on a new phase in its long life, under a Headmaster who could in no way be confused with his predecessors either in style or appearance. Dr David Hudson, a Blackpool man, came here from Hereford Sixth Form College, of which he had been Principal for eight years. He was a graduate of Manchester University, where he had followed his first degree in chemistry with an MSc and a PhD in physical sciences.

Dr Hudson's arrival was welcomed in the Annual Report of the Governors, who met that September. Following the Rev A C Betts, the Chair was now occupied by Mrs M A Savill, with Mr M Reid as Vice Chairman, five parent governors, two teacher governors, five LEA governors, six co-opted governors, and Mrs Janet Firth as Clerk. The governors established committees responsible for finance, staffing, community education, and pupil exclusions. They reported on sport and information services and – as was usual now – published an interesting and impressive list of 1997 school leavers and their universities, colleges and other destinations.

Dr Hudson's approach was plainly announced in the *Chaloner* of 1997, which opened with a message from the new Head, illustrated by a breezy cartoon portrait. In this he said:

> I will be watching how things are done for the first year. My father used to have a saying 'If it's not broke, don't fix it,' which means don't change things that are working until you can make them work better. Mr Forster spent years getting the school to where it is today; it would be foolish to lose this by changing for change's sake.

This commendably cautious approach nevertheless left room for Dr Hudson to introduce changes he felt would benefit the school, in particular those which would equip it to take advantage of the rapidly-developing world of computerisation and the internet.

The first major development was the granting of Technology College Status in June 1998, initiated by the Head and with a careful application worked out by a team of senior staff. This meant a big improvement in the school's finances, the essence of which was that the school had to raise at least £100,000, which would be matched by the government. An income over the next three years was then guaranteed, a third of it going to the primary schools. The school was able to find the basic sum thanks to the generosity of the George A Moore Foundation (£25,000), David Brown, CBE, an old boy of King James's Grammar School (£25,000) and various local firms and individuals.

King James's now had the right to use the Technology Colleges logo and was able to implement various projects, including the opening in October 1999 of a Training Centre. Situated to the right of the main entrance – formerly a kitchen area – this was set up with twenty state-of-the-art computers and the necessary training material. For the first three years it was led by Mr Malcom Jones as Training Manager (now working there free-lance). Originally there was an emphasis on training secondary school teachers, later extended to take in staff from primary schools and employees from any firm or institution. In February 2000 the Training Centre was used for a day-conference for 40 Technology College headteachers from Yorkshire and Humberside.

Although the Training Centre was run quite independently, it was part of the school and, in a sense, showed the way forward. To make every child computer-literate was one of the new Headmaster's objectives. If a new technology was available, then there was every reason for a progressive school to exploit it. Early in 1999, for example, two new science labs came into use (arising from the Capital Project of the school's new status), a business plan for a cyber café was presented by Sixth Formers to the Knaresborough CAP group, pupils conducted a marketing survey for the Knaresborough Regeneration Committee, and £20,000 additional funding for technology was successfully applied for.

Later in 1999 at the National Science Museum, Philippa Forrester (of 'Tomorrow's World') presented three Sixth Formers with the third prize in the Toshiba National STEM project for web page construction, and there was the installation of a £70,000 system of computer smartboards and palm tops. In March 2000 the school produced its

Scroll designed by Peter Kearney, presented to Jochen Haase on his retirement in 1998, after 25 years of organising exchanges with the twin town of Bebra, involving over a thousand pupils.

own CD Rom of Knaresborough to celebrate the millennium, full of information and pictures of the contemporary scene, as well as a look at the past.

Any criticism of this new emphasis on technology had to reckon with the fact that the school was undoubtedly enjoying a good reputation. In the *Sunday Times* (November 1999) list of the top 500 state schools King James's came 275th, and parents were eager to send their children here, with 260 applicants making this their first choice in the year 2000.

As well as the installation of electronic and other modern equipment there were some forward-looking changes to the school buildings. In April 2000 the school received a grant of £1,000 from NDS4 (New Deals for Schools) for the provision of an additional staircase in the Middle School block, and an additional maths classroom was built, partly funded by the LEA. In June 2000 work started on the transformation of the old Headmaster's house into a Sixth Form Centre.

This was opened in October 2001 – exactly a hundred years after Tyack Bake had moved into the new building. After the opening, performed by Cynthia Welbourn, Director of Education, North Yorkshire County Council, visitors were shown round these delightful new premises. More of university standard than the spartan facilities we tend to associate with schools, this Sixth Form Centre combines the classrooms, quiet rooms, and library needed for

The Fun Run of the Millennium, at the crowded start of the 18th successful event.

serious study, with provision for drinks and catering. Though not isolated from the main school, it has a feeling of privacy and independence. And it has been pointed out that it contains no easy chairs, because it is intended as a pleasant work-place rather than a privileged retreat for rest and recreation.

King James's School embarked on the new millennium with many improvements to its buildings and its equipment, particularly in respect of the electronic devices we would expect in a school of Technology College Status. But what of the human beings who made use of these up-to-date facilities?

First of all, academic achievement, as reflected in exam results, was well up to standard. The background to this could be seen in a new kind of publication, the impressive colour *Sixth Form Prospectus*. This opens with a letter from Dr Hudson, in which he pays tribute to the excellent state of the Sixth Form he had taken over, quoting the 1997 A Level results of 92% passes, with 42% at A and B grades. The results in August 2000, giving a very satisfying place in the millenial league table, were 93% A Level passes, with 32% at A or B. GNVQ had a 100% pass rate and GCSE 75% (A to C grades). In 2001, when there were 344 in the Sixth Form, 146 took A Level or A/S Level exams. 90% passed A Level, with 32.4% gaining A or B grades, including two Sixth Formers who were in the country's top five in English literature and economics. The pass rate at GNVQ Level was 82.4%, and GCSE had 69.4%, with five or more passes at A to C grades. It is not surprising that in September 2001 the school was awarded the further distinction of Training School Status, a model of how things should be done, the initial training of teachers being led by Julie Bradley, Assistant Head.

As usual there was provision not only for high flyers but also for the least able children. These continued to be helped by the Special Needs department, being given support in class and/or withdrawal from lessons. In 2001 there were 325 pupils on the SEN (Special Educational Needs) Register. Related to this there is always the problem of integrating children with some physical handicap. King James's could now add to its status as an exemplary school the fact that it had been designated as the school in the Harrogate area which particularly catered for physically disabled pupils within its mainstream education. By 2003 King James's would have provided easy wheelchair access to all areas, with lifts in the Science block, Sixth form Centre and library, and a stairlift not far from the entrance.

Not long after the school had been presented with the Curriculum 2000 Award for its work in the community, several innovations were introduced in the September

The school taking part in the Millennium Pageant, June 2000, with the author introducing three Roman soldiers (Michael James, Lewis Hetherington, Tony Talbot) and an Ancient Briton (Mr Kirkham).

of that year. These included, as a major break with the existing system, a 23 period week, with an early finish at 2.50 on Tuesdays and Thursdays, and a later one, at 3.55, for the other days. Also new was a PSHCE period each week, in which form tutors were responsible for 'Personal, Social, Health and Citizenship Education', including sex education.

A wealth of extra-curricular activities was available, as always. The relationship between the staff and pupils was not simply a matter of teacher and taught, but of friendly adults giving extra time and energy to children who could choose from a range of activities recorded in the *Chaloners* of the late 1990s and the early years of the new millennium. They were noted with appreciation by the governors, many of whom made a point of attending school events. Their Annual Report of November 2000, for example, under the chairmanship of Mr D Talbot, acknowledges the many out-of-school activities and the staff contribution that makes these possible.

Here are a few examples of these activities – all described and illustrated in the *Chaloner*, edited by Annie Rose until 2001, when Eileen Minshall took over:

1998 *Cinderella* (the 1997 Sixth Form pantomime); music successes such as *Yanamamo;* trips concerning art, geography, biology, RE and languages (including the customary visits to Bebra, Boulogne, Normandy and the Ardèche); Book Week, the Fun Run (the first of several when Phil Willis, our local MP, opened the event and presented prizes) and every kind of sport. The most novel activity was one which cashed in on the World Cup. Paul Keogh and Mademoiselle Bourré conducted the opening draw in French, then mixed teams from Year Seven started to compete as representatives of the nations they had adopted. A smattering of each of the languages was taught, supported by the geography and history departments and even Food Technology, which prepared appropriate dishes in a colourful and original week. This *Chaloner* also recorded the swimming distinction of Matthew Jackson, Year 12, U16 national champion for 200m breaststroke.

1999 *Daisy pulls it off* (a crazy comedy about a girls' private school); various music concerts, including a Christmas performance by the handbell team; the well-established

Coat-of-arms of King James's School, registered with the College of Heraldry in 1966 to mark the School's 350th Anniversary. This is how it appears on the original document

May Ball for Year 11; Duke of Edinburgh awards; the celebration of ten years of rural enterprise on the school farm; art trips to Florence and Venice – and the first KJS trans-atlantic school trip, when Year Thirteen students were taken to ski near Boston in the USA by Mr Gordon Ibbotson. This year also saw a celebration of the 25th anniversary of the link with the Brüder-Grimm Schule in Bebra, when 30 German pupils came to spend ten days in school and on excursions.

2000 *Chaloner*. The popular musical *Grease*, playing to packed houses; sessions of painting and sculpture organised by Mr Crawford; a young engineer regional winner and national finalist, Simon Bachelor; the usual range of trips, this time including one to Barcelona, and the exchange visit of French children from a school in Privas, one of whom, interestingly, wrote how impressed she was by the school toilets.

In June 2000 the school, both staff and pupils, made a valuable contribution to the Knaresborough Millennium Pageant, which I had the pleasure of presenting in the ruins of Knaresborough Castle. KJS provided us with Ancient Britons, Roman soldiers, Angles, a Norman knight, King John and the thirteen paupers, Queen Philippa, Richard II, pupils from 1616, and many more, the music being provided by the Senior Wind Band, along with the Knaresborough Silver Band, special items, including an Anthem for Knaresborough, being composed and conducted by Mr Bryan Western, Head of Music.

2001 *Chaloner*. An Alan Ayckbourne play, entirely directed and acted by pupils/students; two evenings of theatre studies presentations by the Sixth Form; the winning of the BBC's Young Chorister of the Year competition by Emily Gray; the annual pantomime, the Senior Citizens Party and a splendid Christmas school dinner put on by the dinner-ladies, with Santa Claus (a second-nature role played by Dr Hudson) distributing sweets. There were science visits, including one to Edinburgh to hear a lecture by Stephen Hawkins, after which it was decided to form the school's first Astronomy Club – and a tangible piece of scientific research in the installation of a photovoltaic panel, opened by Phil Willis, MP, on the wall of the Middle School quad, providing both a practical demonstration and ongoing use of solar energy.

These *Chaloners*, brightened by photographs and pieces of creative verse, now became a standard part of the introductory package of information given to prospective parents and to pupils, teacher applicants and visitors.

Celebration on the School Farm. On Valentine's Day 1998 Molly the sow, with perfect arithmetic, gave birth to a litter of 14 piglets. Holding three of them are Lucy Heywood, Sarah Mulholland and Sarah Wheelhouse.

The opening years of the millennium saw a considerable number of staff changes, with new blood entering the system to replace those who were retiring. Amongst the many newcomers were, for example, Hilary Gee, appointed as the Headmaster's Personal Assistant, Carl Sugden, a new Deputy Head, Paul Sorby, new Head of Maths and Wendy Fraser, Head of Sixth Form – and the namesake of a French teacher here in the 1970s. The leavers with long service in 1998 were first, Bob Hearld, who had been teaching here for an incredible 35 years, most of this time with consistent success as Head of Boys' PE, but since 1990 as a teacher of maths and the school's examinations officer. Brian Fitzgibbon retired after 25 years here as a teacher of metalwork, Year Head, maker of stage sets and props, as well as fund-raiser for the school in Mongegba. Val Heward left after 19 years here, teaching maths and helping with music, to take up a post as Head of Maths at a school in Hull.

In January 1999 the school mourned the death of Mrs Ros Mason, who had taught mainly Food Technology, but since 1989 had been Head of Careers. From the office Mrs Pat Beardsley retired after 13 years service at King James's. In December 1999 Ken Hall, economics, who had been Head of Sixth Form, then, from 1997, Director of Main School, moved to become Deputy Head of a school with something in common, the King James Community College, Bishop Auckland, before becoming Head of Spennymoor School. In 2000 King James's lost one of its well-known personalities in the retirement of Ron Burnett, who had taught art here for 28 years, to say nothing of designing programmes and scenery, and happily playing his trombone, now to be given more time in his Mardi Gras Jazzband.

In 2001 Jan Russell left after teaching geography at King James's for 25 years, as well as serving as a Head of Year and Head of Careers. From the science department Pete Wormald left after 24 years here teaching chemistry and maths, and moved to St Aidan's. Another Aidan, Mr Burbridge, who also had served 24 years, retired after being Head of Economics as well as Head of Sixth Form.

In 2002 the school said goodbye to long-servers such as Peter Whitehead (17 years), Mike Garside (20), Kath Crebbin (26), and Christine Parkin (29). The outstanding retirement in 2002 was that of Don Winspear, an unshakeable pillar of the establishment for 27 years, during which time he had become widely respected as time-tabler, administrator, tour organiser and general overseer. In his speech at a happy farewell lunch provided by the dinner-ladies in the

King James's School Uniform, displayed with a happy smile!

School Hall Mr Winspear paid tribute to former Headmasters, and also to the one he had worked with most recently, who was sitting just in front of him. Referring to Dr Hudson's larger-than-life personality, no less than to his formidable frame, he commented in a nicely-turned compliment: 'You don't get many of *him* to the pound!'

This opinion of the Headmaster was confirmed a couple of months later when the school underwent another Ofsted inspection, between the 9th and 12th of September 2002. The report of the 15 inspectors was just as good as the one delivered six years earlier. Comparing King James's with what it had been in 1996, it was noted that the school was bigger, with 1,726 pupils. The inspectors believed this considerable growth was the result of the school's popularity, and that it was a victim of success in that numbers were 'beginning to put a strain on current levels of accommodation'.

Nevertheless, the increasing numbers had made no difference to the school's standards of attainment in exams, which the inspectors found 'well above the national average':

> Pupils' personal development is significantly enhanced by an ethos which is caring and supportive. Teachers have established a very positive rapport with pupils, which is conductive to effective learning. The school is well led and has a clear sense of shared values and objectives; it provides good value for money.

As the *Knaresborough Post* reported, a key aspect of the success praised in the report was the school's ability to work closely with parents through meetings and formal feedback, including sending out questionnaires on issues ranging from uniforms to security. Illustrating the press report there was a picture of pupils with Dr Hudson and Mrs Estelle Edwards, OBE, Chair of Governors, celebrating the Ofsted result.

Though there are minor criticisms to be found in the Inspection Report of 2002 there is no doubt that King James's, once again, received

Classroom of the future. KJS learners sitting before computers, rather than facing a blackboard.

the highest official praise for every aspect of its work. This is a matter of historical record.

It is fortunately not the business of a historian to do his own Ofsted or make a formal assessment of the success and status of the school. Yet it must be said, as we come to the end of the story so far, that for almost 400 years King James's has served Knaresborough well. And now, after all the chances and changes of the centuries, after all the thousands of children and hundreds of teachers who have come and gone, it is still a valuable asset to the town, and to Yorkshire itself. To say the least, this school is a going concern, adaptable and resilient, with every indication that it will continue to thrive.

In 2003 the school had a total of nearly 1,800 children, 147 teachers, 19 tutors and support staff for Special Needs, 34 other staff, including secretaries, administrative assistants, technicians and caretakers, with Mr C Teeling as Facilities Manager. Last, but not in

any way least, 15 catering staff and 20 cleaning staff – all this a vastly improved provision of personnel when compared with the 1970s.

A good school can never afford to rest on its laurels, as the present Headmaster is well aware. During the closing stages of writing this history Dr Hudson showed me round some of the latest developments. Near the re-styled entrance and spacious reception area he took me into a large classroom, which I remembered as the old

Looking back to the old uniform, mostly supplied for many years by an old boy of KJGS, Howard Bell. The cap on the right was introduced in 1958

Headmasters of King James's School

Mr Frank Brewin (1955-1975)

Mr John Moreton (1975-1981)

Mr John Forster (1981-1997)

Dr David Hudson (from 1997)

The multicoloured carpet in the corridor of the new Year Seven area (2003).

KJGS physics lab, then the library. 'This', said the Headmaster, 'is the class-room of the future'.

I was impressed by the gleaming array of brand-new computers, all round the walls... But, as an old teacher, I was looking for a blackboard, and instinctively feeling for my bit of chalk.

'No need for blackboards', said the technophile Head, and proceeded to explain how electronic gadgetry could instantly present a word or illustration on the individual screens.

Next he showed me the library (once the school's hall/gym), which was in process of being extended to occupy three floors. I thought with unease of so-called paperless schools – with the kids exclusively engaged in tapping keyboards and manipulating mice – and I was thankful that at King James's there was still a place for real books.

Finally, the Head showed me the new area used by Year Seven, the young beginners for so long known as First Years. They now had their own cosy playground, just outside, complete with seats and shrubs. Most noticeable was their new carpet, extending in vivid, multicoloured stripes all along the corridor.

'This,' said Dr Hudson, 'is a symbol. It's the gateway to the future'.

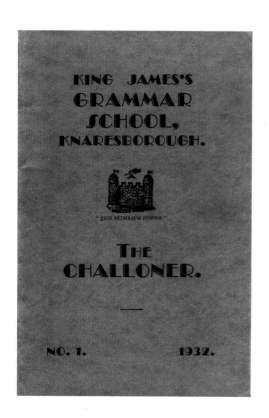

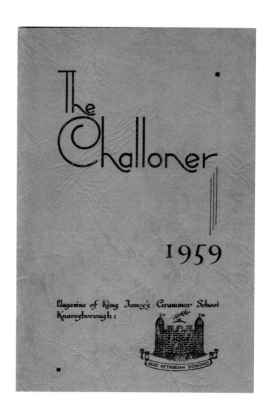

The school magazine, showing the first issue in 1932, with glimpses of Desmond Gill as Hamlet (1959) and music of the school song by Mr Maurice Armsby, in use from 1968.

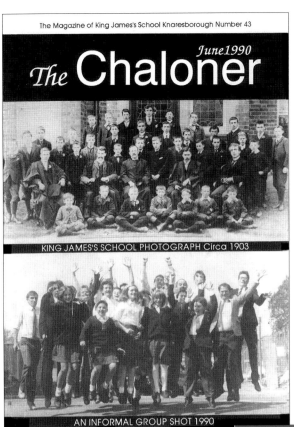

KING JAMES'S SCHOOL PHOTOGRAPH Circa 1903

AN INFORMAL GROUP SHOT 1990

The revived school magazine in 1990, with a recent colour version, including modern art.

A Compact Chronology

1603	King James the Sixth of Scotland is crowned James the First of England
1605	Gunpowder Plot attempts to destroy the King
1611	King James's Authorised Version of the Bible
1616	King James grants permission to the Rev Dr Robert Chaloner to found a Free Grammar School in Knaresborough. Chaloner sets out 24 school rules as his Ordinances and Lawes. House near Parish Church given by Peter Benson
1617	Thomas Crosbie, first Master of King James's. Paid £20 per annum
1621	Death of Dr Chaloner, Canon of Windsor, Rector of Amersham, Buckinghamshire
1625	Death of King James. Succeeded by his son, Charles I
1642	Civil War begins
1644	Knaresborough Castle taken by Parliamentarians, but Thomas Bateson (Royalist) continues as Master of King James's
1653	Henry Doughty, Master of King James's (until 1675)
1660	Restoration of monarchy under Charles II
1688	Sir Henry Goodrick of Ribston Hall proclaims William III
1717	Birth of John Metcalf, 'Blind Jack of Knaresborough'
1734	Eugene Aram sets up school in Knaresborough
1741	Rebuilding of original Grammar School on same site
1765	Thomas Richardson's Charity School, High Street
1785	Sunday Schools started in Knaresborough, with 500 children
1788	Death of Rev Thomas Collins, Vicar since 1735
1800	Rev James Neale, Master of King James's. Later absconds with school papers
1814	Boys' National School, Castle Yard
1815	Battle of Waterloo. Wesleyan Chapel, Gracious Street (later school)
1823	Knaresborough Improvement Commissioners formed
1837	Girls' National School, Castle Yard
1850	Thomas Idell, Master of King James's
1851	Railway Viaduct rebuilt after collapse
1878	Robert Harvie, Master of King James's. Still paid £20 per annum
1895	Urban District Council. Richardson's amalgamates with Grammar School
1896	H J Tyack Bake, Head Master. Salary increased to £100 per annum
1901	School moves to York Road site, opened by Lord Harewood
1905	Grammar School closes down, because of lack of pupils
1908	Re-opens as Knaresborough Rural Secondary School under G W Hefford
1912	C W H Greaves, Head Master
1914-18	First World War
1915	Council School moves from Gracious Street to Stockwell Road
1922	A S ('Sam') Robinson, Headmaster of King James's

1926	King James's officially restored to Grammar School status
1932	First issue of school magazine. New buildings for Boroughbridge Secondary School
1933	Grammar School extensions opened by Lord Harewood
1939-45	Second World War. RAF heroes, 'Bunny' Clayton and 'Ginger' Lacey
1950	Sam Robinson retires. D J Stevens appointed Headmaster
1955	Frank Brewin appointed Headmaster
1964	New hall, science block, gym, library etc opened by Lord James
1966	350th anniversary celebrations. School coat-of-arms registered
1968	Start of extensions and new building for Comprehensive School
1971	King James's School opens (7th September) combining King James's Grammar School with the Secondary Modern Schools of Knaresborough and Boroughbridge
1972	Official opening by HRH the Duchess of Kent (29th February)
1974	First exchange with Brüder-Grimm Schule, Bebra
1975	Sudden death of Mr Brewin (13th February)
1975	Mr J E W Moreton appointed Headmaster. Changes in pastoral system, setting etc
1981	Mr J R Forster appointed Headmaster
1983	King James's School founded in Mongegba, Sierra Leone. First Fun Run
1990	Revival of school magazine, the *Chaloner*
1995	King James's receives Investors in People Award
1996	Ofsted Inspection. First class Report
1997	Mr John Forster retires
1997	Dr David Hudson appointed Headmaster
1998	King James's attains Technology College Status
2000	Millennium Pageant. CD Rom of Knaresborough
2001	Sixth Form Centre opens (former Headmaster's house)
2002	Ofsted Inspection. Another first class Report
2003	Entrance and library enlarged. Publication of *King James's School, Knaresborough 1616-2003*, to mark the 400th anniversary of the accession of King James to the throne of England

The last bell. For many years this old handbell, shaken at strategic points by prefects, regulated the school day. It was kept as a memento by the Caretaker, Albert Scurrah, who presented it to the school when he retired in 1968, having served here since 1928.